Sugarloaf

Very best wishes
to Robin —

Melonie Choukas-
Bradley

Sugarloaf

The Mountain's History, Geology, and Natural Lore

Melanie Choukas-Bradley
Illustrations by Tina Thieme Brown

UNIVERSITY OF VIRGINIA PRESS
Charlottesville and London

Publication of this book was assisted by a grant from Sugarloaf
Regional Trails.

This book was developed for publication for the University of
Virginia Press by the Center for American Places.
www.americanplaces.org

University of Virginia Press
Printed in the United States of America on acid-free paper
First published 2003

9 8 7 6 5 4 3

Frontispiece: Sugarloaf Mountain, view from Comus

LIBRARY OF CONGRESS CATALOGING-IN-PUBLICATION DATA
Choukas-Bradley, Melanie
    Sugarloaf: the mountain's history, geology, and natural lore /
Melanie Choukas-Bradley ; illustrations by Tina Thieme Brown.
        p. cm.
    Includes bibliographical references (p.   ) and index.
        ISBN 0-8139-2168-6 (pbk. : alk. paper)
        1. Sugar Loaf Mountain (Md.) —Guidebooks.   I. Brown, Tina
Thieme, 1952– II. Center for American Places.   III. Title.

F187.F8 C45 2003
917.52'87—dc21   2002154223

13-digit ISBN: 978-0-8139-2168-6

*For Jim, Sophie, and Jesse Choukas-Bradley
and Jim, Jacob, and Josh Brown*

Contents

Preface

This book is for everyone who loves Sugarloaf Mountain. As the only accessible mountain close to Washington, D.C., Sugarloaf is a national treasure. This small mountain, a National Natural Landmark, serves as a year-round refuge for seekers of solitude and natural beauty. The pleasingly curved profile that rests so lightly on the horizon northwest of the nation's capital is, upon close inspection, a delightfully rocky, wooded landscape. Nearly fifteen miles of interlocking hiking trails entice explorers of all ages.

At 1,282 feet, Sugarloaf would hardly register on a map of the Rockies or even the nearby Blue Ridge, but because it stands alone, and in such close proximity to Washington and Baltimore, Sugarloaf dominates the landscape for miles around and is a favored destination for nearly a quarter of a million visitors annually. If you are among them, whether you have come to hike the network of trails, circle the base on your bicycle, or just sit quietly at East View or West View drawing inspiration from the farmland below, you probably have fallen under the spell of this place.

It happened to Gordon Strong more than a century ago. A young lawyer and property manager, the son of a wealthy Chicago industrialist, Strong fell in love with Sugarloaf and spent his lifetime purchasing it woodlot by woodlot. He lived there for many years with his wife, Louise Strong, and then left his land in the care of a private trust charged with preserving the mountain and keeping it open to the public. Strong so loved Sugarloaf that he thwarted the plans of two of the twentieth century's most formidable personalities. According to local lore, when President Franklin Delano Roosevelt, a frequent visitor to Sugarloaf, tried to obtain the mountain as a White House retreat, Strong declined, sending Roosevelt farther north to the Catoctins and the present-day Camp David. When Frank Lloyd Wright revealed his commissioned design for a summit observatory and entertainment complex to Gordon Strong, Strong decided against the mammoth structure, and a disappointed Wright went back to the drawing board. He ultimately adapted elements of his Sugarloaf design for the Guggenheim Museum in New York City.

This book tells the story of Gordon Strong's legacy and many other tales that link Sugarloaf with the Indian settlements of the past and the birth and preservation of the nation. The family of Thomas Johnson, the first governor of Maryland and the man who nominated George Washington to be commander in chief of the Continental Army, owned businesses at the foot of the mountain that were fueled by charcoal from Sugarloaf-area trees. One of the first major glassworks in the nation and an early primitive, horse-powered railroad were constructed and operated from the base of Sugarloaf Mountain. During the Civil War, a massive incursion of Confederate troops into Union territory was spotted from the signal station at the summit of Sugarloaf. Days later, the battle of Antietam took place nearby, the battle that still stands as America's bloodiest day.

Sugarloaf holds the distinction of being the only mountain in the Maryland Piedmont. Composed of hard, erosion-resistant rock, Sugarloaf held fast for an estimated 14 million years while the countryside eroded around it. Such a mountain left standing alone is called a monadnock. Today, Sugarloaf gently commands the horizon between the historic cities of Leesburg, Virginia, and Frederick, Maryland. On the clearest days, Sugarloaf can be seen from the towers of the Washington National Cathedral and the Washington Monument. Rising from a rolling landscape of farms and villages, Sugarloaf's wooded slopes are crowned by cliffs composed of pink and gray-white quartzite. From the open summit, one looks out over pastures and fields of corn, soybean, and wheat, all part of a vanishing rural landscape unencumbered by suburban development. It's easy to see why the Sugarloaf region has long been a mecca for artists and poets. On the mountain's woodland trails, several hundred plant species and a myriad of birds and other wildlife offer quiet communion with nature throughout the seasons. Sugarloaf is a rejuvenating destination for anyone wanting a break from the harried pace of contemporary life.

How to Use This Book

This book is designed for the day hiker, the naturalist, and the armchair historian. For information about visiting Sugarloaf and exploring its natural wonders, consult the introduction, where we also describe Gordon Strong's philosophy about the importance of creating and maintaining a close connection with nature. Refer to chapters 1 and 2 for information about Sugarloaf's geologic and historic past. In chapter 3 you will find detailed guides to Sugarloaf's trail network, with practical tips about preparing for your mountain outing. The trail guides include many descriptions of the plant and animal life you will find along the way. In chapter 4 we provide an overview of the native and naturalized herbaceous and woody plants growing at Sugarloaf. (For a comprehensive description of individual species, consult our forthcoming companion volume, *An Illustrated Guide to Eastern Woodland Wildflowers and Trees: 350 Plants Observed at Sugarloaf Mountain, Maryland.*) In chapter 5 you will find descriptions of Sugarloaf's birds, mammals, reptiles, and amphibians; in chapter 6 we share some of the seasonal journeys you can experience in Sugarloaf country; and in chapter 7 we discuss the conservation challenges facing this rural area lying so close to a rapidly expanding metropolis.

We hope that this book enhances your visits to Sugarloaf Mountain and increases your sensitivity to the importance of its unspoiled habitats. We have spent many years exploring Sugarloaf, and we have come to appreciate the beauty of the changing light and shadow on its rocks. Our love for the wildflowers and trees has deepened over time as we anticipate familiar seasonal events and are delighted by unexpected ones. When you visit Sugarloaf, stay long enough to let the mountain work its magic on you. Sugarloaf is the crown jewel of Maryland's historic rural Piedmont. Come to know it well and learn what you can do to help preserve the farms and villages you see from its summit.

We wish to thank the many people and organizations who assisted us in the creation of this book. Sugarloaf Regional Trails, founded by the late Frederick "Fritz" Gutheim, supported the project with generous grants. Tina received a grant from the Arts Council of Montgomery County, Maryland. The Center for American Places, under the remarkable leadership of president George F. Thompson and with the able assistance of editor Randall B. Jones, brought the project to fruition. Director Penelope Kaiserlian and the talented staff at the University of Virginia Press are responsible for the volume you hold in your hands. Lynne M. Bonenberger edited the manuscript. Our close friend, botanist Cris Fleming, was invaluable in the field and as a tireless consultant and botanical editor. Stronghold's executive secretary/treasurer, David F. Webster, and its many employees past and present generously shared their time and knowledge of Sugarloaf. Special thanks go to Susan Dunn and former superintendents Robert Holland, Ben Smart, and Mark Swick. We also are grateful to the late Karl C. Jonas, chairman of the Stronghold board, for his support. Longtime Sugarloaf activist Minny Pohlmann gave us her undying moral support. The Audubon Naturalist Society's executive director, Neal Fitzpatrick, and former *Washington Post* garden columnist and author Charles Fenyvesi were very supportive.

Local naturalists who contributed time and expertise to the project include birders Anne Sturm, Rex Sturm, and Chet Anderson, botanists Kerrie Kyde and Carole Bergmann, and science teacher Joyce Bailey. Mike Choukas, Melanie's father, gave birding advice, and Melanie's nephew, Nick Jones, helped with botany. Pete DiLonardo advised us on cartography. Judy Daniel, Dolores Milmoe, and Ed Thompson provided information about farmland conservation. Cynthia Shauer Langstaff, Dwight Bradley, and Jim Reger advised us on geology. Research librarians at the Historical Society of Frederick County, Maryland, and the Montgomery County Historical Society assisted us. Charles T. Jacobs provided invaluable information on Civil War history. Peg Coleman, Robert Kapsch, John Baines, Fawn A. E. Foerster, Glenn Cumings, Tom Proctor, Susan Cooke Soderberg, and the late Jacqueline Nichols shared information about local history. Heather Germaine described Sugarloaf's inclusion in the National Natural Landmarks Program. Jim Choukas-Bradley helped to interpret Gordon Strong's will and related documents. Jeffrey Tishman shared information on Olympic fencing coach François Darrieulat. Jeff Daniels was an ace computer adviser, copyeditor, and proofreader. Sophie Choukas-Bradley also helped with proofreading.

We thank our many friends who tramped the trails with us, including Terrie Daniels, Dalis Davidson, Ellen Gordon, Ellen Gordon Gordon, Lisa Lindberg, Laura Rounds, and Bev Thoms. Their sensitive observations enhanced this book. Many other friends inspired us and cheered us on. Melanie thanks fellow writers Ellie Anderson, Helene Brenner, Linda Goldman, Larry Letich, Jane Loeffler, Harriot Manley, and Tim Ward for their camaraderie and helpful comments. And last, but certainly not least, thanks to Jim, Jacob, and Josh Brown and Jim, Sophie, and Jesse Choukas-Bradley, and to our extended families, for their loving support.

Sugarloaf

Entrance to Sugarloaf (The Sugarloaf Mountain Gate)

Visiting Sugarloaf

A Popular Mountain

With an elevation of less than thirteen hundred feet, Sugarloaf is no Everest or Denali. Still, it is beloved by those who are drawn to it each year, many of them frequent, longtime visitors. The only real mountain in Maryland's Piedmont, Sugarloaf, which lies primarily in Frederick County, straddles the border of Montgomery County and lies some thirty-five miles northwest of Washington, D.C., and fifty miles west of Baltimore. Sugarloaf is a thirty-three-hundred-acre privately owned park that is open to the public from dawn to dusk year-round. The curved mountain profile was christened with the name Sugarloaf or Pain de Sucre by early European explorers and settlers who were reminded of their crystallized, cone-shaped loaves of sugar.

The mountain is home to several hundred plant species, including some that are rare and threatened. For the purple-fringed and yellow-fringed orchids, which are classified as threatened species in Maryland, Sugarloaf is critical habitat. Sugarloaf's trees and wildflowers provide not only year-round beauty to the visitors who come to hike, picnic, and rest their world-weary souls, but also food and shelter for wildlife, which is being forced out of surrounding land by encircling development. The pristine beauty of this small yet cherished mountain is due to Mother Nature—and to the vision of one persistent man.

Gordon Strong's Legacy

If Gordon Strong could return to Sugarloaf Mountain today, more than a century after he first laid eyes on it and half a century since his death, he would find a place even more pristine than the mountain that, according to local legend, he first fell in love with on a bicycle trip as a young man. (See chapter 2 for more on Gordon Strong.)

The wealthy native Midwesterner who spent a lifetime purchasing the badly deforested Sugarloaf piece by piece, and then drafting a preservation plan for its future, would probably be among those who anticipate the spring blooming of the mountain's lady's slippers and the return of the musically ethereal wood thrush. During the years he spent on Sugarloaf, building and living in his elegant mansion near the base, Gordon Strong came to believe that a close connection with nature was, next to human companionship, the most rewarding and nourishing experience a person could have.

Speaking for himself and his wife, Louise, with whom he shared a passion for the small mountain they called home for many years, Strong wrote: "In our lives, beauty (whereby, we almost always mean out-of-doors beauty) has ranked second only to those close to us in human association and affection." Strong even speculated on the likelihood that an appreciation for natural beauty could inspire "moral betterment."

"We have no personal experience, no observation of others, on which to base anything like a conclusion," he wrote. "But we incline to believe that, when anyone stands on the summit of the mountain, the sheer cliff hanging over the wooded slopes below, looking out over the peaceful and lovely Frederick valley, and showing Catoctin and Blue Ridge rising to meet the lowering sun, for a moment at least he experiences an inspiration, a moral uplift."[1]

Many suns have lowered over the Frederick Valley since Gordon Strong put those words to paper, and the view from the summit of Sugarloaf has continued to inspire and uplift its witnesses.

A visit to Sugarloaf can include so much more than a day's hike. True, the network of nearly fifteen miles of trails provides excellent hiking through woods and over open, rocky terrain. The mountain's trails skirt delightful streams and climb to dramatic viewpoints. Visitors of all ages and fitness levels will find places to explore.

Sugarloaf Mountain summit, looking west over the Monocacy River Valley

But the smooth pink rocks seem to say, "Stop and sit awhile"; the spring wildflowers and autumn leaves invite contemplation; and when the wood thrush sings or the whip-poor-will calls out from the trees, who could fail to pause and listen?

Sugarloaf is a place to slow down and become a part of the natural world. For children, it is the wild backyard that rarely exists behind the house.

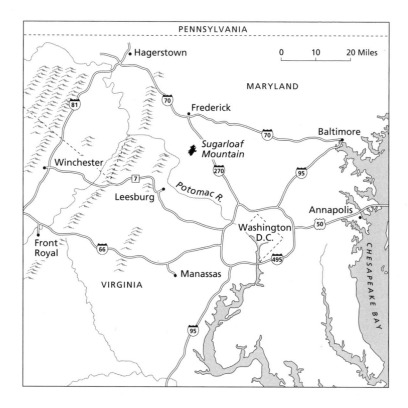

Directions and Visitor Information

Sugarloaf Mountain is open to the public, at this writing free of charge, from sunrise to sunset daily. The mountain is located west of the village of Comus, northwest of the town of Barnesville, and northeast of the town of Dickerson. From Washington, D.C., take I-495 to I-270. Turn south (right) on Route 109 (Barnesville, Hyattstown exit) and drive three miles to the intersection of Comus Road. Turn right on Comus Road (west) and drive just under two and a half miles to the base of Sugarloaf. From Baltimore's I-695, take I-70 west to Route 75. Go south on Route 75 to Route 355. Turn left on Route 355 (south) and drive partway through Hyattstown. Turn right on Route 109 (south) and drive to Comus Road. Go right on Comus Road to the mountain base.

A limited amount of parking is available at the mountain base, with additional parking up the mountain road at East View and West View. Picnic tables and portable toilets are located at East View, West View, and just beyond the wooden buildings flanking the mountain road near the base. Alcohol is not permitted. Trails may be accessed from the mountain base, East View, West View, or Mount Ephraim Road. Trail maps are available in holders at East View, West View, and on the side of the wooden building on the left just past the mountain

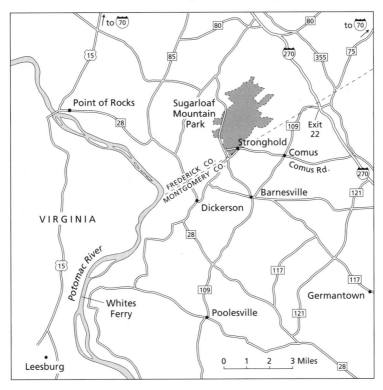

gate. (See chapter 3 for detailed trail descriptions.) As of this writing, mountain biking is allowed only on the Yellow Trail on weekdays from May through November. The Yellow Trail is designated as a year-round hiking and horseback-riding trail. All plants and wildlife at the mountain must remain unharmed. Collecting is prohibited. Sugarloaf is privately owned and administered by the nonprofit Stronghold corporation. For more information, or to inquire about renting the Strong Mansion for weddings and special parties or volunteering for trail maintenance, please contact: Stronghold, Inc., 7901 Comus Rd., Dickerson, Md. 20842 (301-874-2024 or 301-869-7846).

The Surroundings

To the east, south, and northeast of Sugarloaf lies a ninety-thousand-plus-acre Agricultural Reserve designed to limit commercial and residential development and support farming and outdoor recreation. This open space comprises a pleasing patchwork of farms, punctuated by the charming historic villages of Comus, Barnesville, Boyds, Dickerson, Beallsville, and Hyattstown. To the northwest lies the town of Buckeystown and beyond that the historic city of Frederick.

Unpaved, tree-shaded rural roads nearly encircle the mountain. The mountain is flanked by Sugarloaf Mountain Road on the east side, Mount Ephraim Road to the west, and Peters Road on the north (accessed by paved connecting roads). A profusion of spring wildflowers and dramatic autumn foliage are among the rewards of exploring these roads by mountain bike.

Two small creeks originate on the western slopes of Sugarloaf: Furnace Branch and Bear Branch. The former flows into the Monocacy River not far from its confluence with the Potomac, and the latter flows into Bennett Creek, which skirts the northern slopes of the mountain.

Immediately west and southwest of Stronghold property lies the Monocacy Natural Resources Management Area (see p. 65 for a brief description). Many other nearby natural and historic areas invite exploration, including the C&O Canal along the Potomac, Little Bennett and Black Hill regional parks, Seneca Creek State Park, Gambrill State Park, and Catoctin Mountain Park. A little farther afield are

Washington Monument State Park along the Appalachian Trail on South Mountain, and the historic West Virginia towns of Harpers Ferry and Shepherdstown. Several Civil War battlefields are within easy driving distance of Sugarloaf, including the Monocacy National Battlefield and the Antietam National Battlefield.

1 The Geology of Sugarloaf Mountain

Sugarloaf Mountain is a monadnock, a mountain that stands alone after the surrounding countryside has eroded away around it. Sugarloaf is made up of very hard, erosion-resistant rock called quartzite. The summit of the mountain is composed of a quartzite slab that may be as much as 200 feet thick. Quartzite is metamorphosed sandstone—formed from sand laid down millions of years ago when the region was under water, and subsequently folded and altered by high pressure and temperature. Sugarloaf stands 800 feet above the surrounding countryside to the east, and slightly higher above the Frederick Valley to the west. On the western side of the mountain, 150-foot cliffs rise above piles of fallen rock called talus.[1]

Sugarloaf is the only mountain in the Maryland Piedmont, and its rock is similar to the rock that makes up the longer ridges of Maryland's Blue Ridge, which you see when you look to the west from Sugarloaf's summit. Catoctin Mountain (the first ridge you see) and South Mountain (the farther ridge) are formed largely of Weverton Quartzite, rock that was metamorphosed from sandstone laid down more than five hundred million years ago and then dramatically uplifted when the great continental plates collided to form the supercontinent called Pangaea. Sugarloaf's quartzite may have begun forming at the same time or even earlier.

Cynthia Shauer Langstaff, a geologist living in the Sugarloaf area, described what conditions might have been like during the Early Cambrian geologic era when the sands that would ultimately make up Sugarloaf Mountain were first deposited by the waters of a vast ocean called Iapetus: "They were very clean, well-sorted sandstones, perhaps laid down on an old beach—sort of the Cape Cod of the Cambrian. The sea was fairly shallow. The first skeletal remains appear in the Cambrian but there were no fish or significant land plants yet.

"I have seen ripple marks on Sugarloaf that could be sand wavelets made by currents on an ancient beach," said Langstaff. "Imagine seeing ripples made on a beach millions of years ago that look like the ones you see today at the Eastern Shore." Starting about 450 million years ago, a series of geologic events metamorphosed the sandstone. During the last of these, 280–330 million years ago, the African plate slammed into North America. In Langstaff's words: "The two continents met in a wreck that crumpled the crust like a car caught between a wall and an eighteen-wheeler. Huge jagged mountains rose up along fault scarps. High temperatures and pressures resulted in chemical and physical changes in the rocks." As the Sugarloaf sandstones were heated and compressed, the pores between grains closed and the rock was cemented into a solid quartzite. Many geologists believe the Blue Ridge mountains may once have been as high as or higher than the Rockies. Millions of years of erosion have worn them down to their present-day elevations. Over time, the great continental plates have drifted apart, resulting in the Atlantic Ocean. This continental drift continues today.

Sugarloaf Mountain took shape over an estimated fourteen million years, according to some geologic calculations, as the forces of wind and water wore away the less resistant rock around Sugarloaf's hard quartzite. In what Langstaff called "the final sculpting episode," "grain by grain, the mass of the mountains was transported out to the Coastal Plain and to the ocean basin beyond. The softer phyllitic materials eroded faster, and the harder quartzite remained," forming the mountain we know today.[2]

Maryland is rather neatly divided (from west to east) into several physiographic regions: the high Allegheny Plateau of far western Maryland; then, moving eastward, the Ridge and Valley (or Valley and

Ridge) province; the Great Valley (Maryland's extension of the Shenandoah Valley); the Blue Ridge; the Piedmont (Sugarloaf's region); and the Coastal Plain.

The Allegheny Plateau is a high plateau with narrow valleys that forms part of the drainage divide in the eastern United States. It includes the highlands of West Virginia and Garrett County, Maryland. Waters flowing east from the Allegheny Plateau enter the Atlantic Ocean; rivers and streams running west eventually flow into the Gulf of Mexico.

The Ridge and Valley province to the east of the Allegheny Plateau is a series of parallel ridges and valleys, formed when the African plate collided with North America. The force of the collision and subsequent uplift folded and fractured the land of the Ridge and Valley province.

Just east lies the Great Valley (Shenandoah in Virginia, Hagerstown in Maryland), part of a relatively open landscape that runs from northeast to southwest for hundreds of miles. This is traditional farming country with rich soil. The Great Valley also has served as an important migration and transportation corridor throughout human history.

East of the Great Valley lies the Blue Ridge, running from Pennsylvania to Georgia and northern Alabama. Catoctin and South Mountains, the closest ridges viewed from Sugarloaf, comprise the Blue Ridge in Maryland. In addition to quartzite, Maryland's Blue Ridge Mountains are composed of several other rock types, including the metamorphic rocks phyllite, gneiss, and metabasalt. A rock called metarhyolite (or simply rhyolite) would serve generations of Indians who traveled to Catoctin and South Mountains to use it to create spear points.

The next province to the east is Sugarloaf's region, the Piedmont (French for "foot" of the "mountain," or foothill), a rolling countryside some thirty to fifty miles wide running east of the Appalachian Mountains (including the Blue Ridge) from eastern Canada, New York, and New England to Alabama. The often pastoral look of this hilly terrain belies its violent geologic past: it was here that the great continental collision, and earlier geologic events, caused the most fracturing, folding, and cooking. Natural history writers Cristol Fleming, Marion Blois Lobstein, and Barbara Tufty described the scene over geologic time:

> The geology of the Piedmont is complex, for throughout hundreds of millions of years the ancient bedrock has been changed by heat and pressure of numerous geological events. As continents collided, the old ocean floors were shoved up, heated, folded over many times, and pushed westward, one on top of the other, like slabs of ice shoved by the wind and water along the edges of a frozen river. When these folds and slabs of ancient ocean bottom cooled, they solidified into metamorphosed rock, primarily gneiss, schist, and quartzite, which are interspersed in local areas with metamorphic igneous rocks such as soapstone and serpentinite. Molten magma repeatedly pushed between the folds and fractures, then cooled, hardened, and crystallized into the granite and basalt rocks we see today.[3]

In Maryland, Sugarloaf Mountain crowns the rolling Piedmont landscape; the mountain is the only height of land in the state's Piedmont to withstand the forces of erosion over geologic time. Looking southward from the summit of Sugarloaf you can see on the horizon Virginia's Bull Run Mountains, another erosion-resistant height of land.

Continuing east from Maryland's Piedmont region, one reaches the Atlantic Coastal Plain. The division between the hilly Piedmont and the flat Coastal Plain is called the Fall Line because of the many waterfalls and rapids occurring along its length. Washington, D.C., Baltimore, Philadelphia, and Richmond are among the cities at the fall line, the last easily navigable stretch of river when traveling upstream from the Atlantic. The Coastal Plain is made up of eroded rock and soil washed down over millions of years from the higher western terrain.

From the summit of Sugarloaf, a good sweep of regional geology is visible: the still largely rural Piedmont of Maryland and Virginia stretching north, south, and east and the Blue Ridge Mountains of Maryland and Virginia in the west. From Sugarloaf's summit, the Blue Ridge is almost always the characteristic bluish hue that is traditionally associated with the ridge's famous summer haze. The course of the Potomac River can be traced as it divides the two states, cutting through the mountains at Point of Rocks, Maryland, and then flowing in a southeasterly direction to the Fall Line at the nation's capital.

2 The History of Sugarloaf Mountain

The small monadnock near the confluence of the Potomac and Monocacy Rivers has been a focal point for hundreds of generations who have hunted, traded, settled, and farmed in this region. During the past several centuries Sugarloaf Mountain and its surroundings have inspired arts and industries of many kinds. Human habitation of the region reaches back at least several thousand years.

Indian Habitation of the Region

As the Ice Age ended some ten to twelve thousand years ago, aboriginal Americans hunted for mastodons and mammoths across the cool grasslands of the Monocacy River Valley. These early Americans of the Paleoindian period left behind fluted projectile points that they had used for hunting. When the earth warmed and forests sprouted from the grasslands, the mastodons and mammoths disappeared and were replaced by deer and other smaller mammals. During the Archaic period (8000–1000 B.C.) Indians discovered that the hard, partially metamorphosed igneous rock called metarhyolite or simply rhyolite, found in the Catoctin Mountains just west of Sugarloaf (and also in South Mountain, the next ridge over), made excellent spear points for hunting. These peoples also gathered summer berries, fall nuts, and other plentiful fruits. They built rock fish weirs (some of which are still visible during low water) in the Monocacy and Potomac Rivers to catch the abundant fish.[1]

By the time European adventurers traveled up the Potomac during the early seventeenth century, Indians (including the hospitable Piscataway) had long been settled in villages along area rivers and streams where they grew crops and continued to exploit the region's plentiful game. The Potomac Indians of the woodland period (1000 B.C.–A.D.1600) had become traders, exchanging furs, food, arrowheads, and other resources far and wide.

As Frederick "Fritz" Gutheim (who lived at the base of Sugarloaf for many years) pointed out in his 1949 classic *The Potomac:* "The very name Potomac in the Algonkin tongue is a verbal noun meaning 'something brought,' and as a designation for a place, 'where something is brought,' or, more freely, 'trading place.' Living, as they did, on one of the great natural trade routes east and west through the mountains, north and south along the fall line, with a highly developed and specialized culture, it was inevitable that the natives of this section should be great traders."[2]

Although trade between the natives and early Europeans developed and flourished for decades, the seventeenth century was a time of turmoil in the Potomac Valley, as the Piscataway were betrayed by the English colonists whom they befriended and hostilities broke out with the more warlike Susquehannoc and Seneca tribes who continued to travel and hunt in the region. By the mid-eighteenth century most Indians were gone from the area, pushed farther to the north and west or dead from European-borne disease.

However, as Gutheim observed, their legacy survived their tragic disappearance: "The Indians of the Potomac valley had a powerful influence on white settlement and subsequent white culture. Indian forms of agriculture, construction, and language, and even forms of government and oratory, were silently absorbed into white settlements all over the Americas. In the Potomac we can see the introduction of specific plants (corn, tobacco, potatoes), new words (hominy, opossum, succotash, wigwam), a new diet. From the first white settlement a new civilization began to be born."[3]

European Exploration and Settlement

Some of the first surviving written and visual records of Sugarloaf Mountain date to the early eighteenth century when two Swiss prospectors explored the Sugarloaf area and made maps of the region. Franz Louis Michel's 1707 map showed Sugarloaf sketched in near the confluence of the river Quattaro (the Monocacy) and the Potomac. After searching for mineral resources in the mountains to the west, Michel settled at the mouth of the Monocacy (near the present-day Monocacy Aqueduct). Here he was joined by a French explorer and trader named Martin Chartier, who had spent decades exploring the Mississippi Valley with LaSalle and who was married to a Shawnee woman.

Baron Christoph von Graffenried heard about the region and its promise of silver mines from his Swiss countryman Michel. Von Graffenried came to the New World with land patents from the English government granting him one hundred thousand acres along the Neuse River in North Carolina and mining rights in Virginia, Maryland, and Pennsylvania. After founding the settlement of New Bern and coming within an inch of his life at the hands of the Tuscarora Indians in North Carolina, von Graffenried traveled north in 1712 hoping to locate silver mines. He never found silver, and he left the Sugarloaf region suspecting Michel had deceived him about its existence and whereabouts.[4] However, he left behind a written record of the mountain and its surroundings:

[W]e visited those beautiful spots of the country, those enchanted islands in the Potomac River above the falls. And from there, on our return, we ascended a high mountain standing alone in the midst of a vast flat stretch of country, called because of its form Sugar Loaf which means in French pain de sucre, taking with us a surveyor . . . named Martin Charetier, and some savages.

. . . We discovered from this height three chains of mountains, the last higher than the one before, somewhat distant and a very fine valley between the first ranges. After we had come down again from this mountain to a place at the foot where there was a very fine spring and good soil, we went to Martin Charetier's where we were lodged and treated after the Indian fashion.[5]

This "good soil" attracted European settlers who found the fertile ground, plentiful water, and available timber hospitable for homesteads and farms. German and Scots-Irish settlers poured in from southeastern Pennsylvania, bringing with them resourcefulness, thrift, and the desire for religious freedom. English settlers also moved up from the tidewater region of the Coastal Plain with their established tobacco culture and its dependence on slave labor. Indian trails running southeast to northwest evolved into the "Great Road" by 1750. This thoroughfare, the current-day Maryland Route 355, which runs through Hyattstown and skirts the northern slopes of Sugarloaf, connected the tobacco port of Georgetown with Frederick. As the authors of *Circling Historic Landscapes* explained, the Great Road was to play a significant role in American history:

> General Edward Braddock's troops rode this path in April 1755 to Braddock's disastrous defeat and death by the French and Indians near present-day Pittsburgh. George Washington traveled it in 1791. It carried fresh troops and supplies from the West during the Revolution and served Federal forces sent to put down the Whiskey Rebellion in western Pennsylvania in 1794. The establishment of the nation's capital in Washington in 1800 and the development of agriculture and industry in the western settlements enhanced the importance of the Great Road. It attained even more significance as an extension of the federally-funded National Road, which was pushed from Cumberland to the Ohio by 1818, and later to St. Louis.[6]

During the nineteenth century two presidents traveling the road to their inaugurations stopped to spend the night in Hyattstown: Andrew Jackson in 1829 and James Polk in 1845. However illustrious the Great Road's history, during its early years it was known for being rutted, muddy in wet weather, and dusty in dry. According to *The History of Hyattstown* by Dona Cuttler and Michael Dwyer: "[T]he road was used by huckster[s], travelers and tobacco farmers rolling their product to market. Herds of animals were driven on the road and tolls were eventually set up to help offset the cost of maintenance in various sections. The more wear and tear you caused to the road surface, the higher the toll."[7]

George Washington had great visions for another major thoroughfare: the Potomac River. His Potowmack Company removed river rocks and built skirting canals, hoping to make the river navigable to Cumberland. These dreams would never pan out quite as Washington envisioned, but one of the friends and colleagues with whom he shared his ideas would, with his large family, make a significant impact on the Sugarloaf Mountain region.

The Johnson Family and Sugarloaf Mountain

Thomas Johnson was the first governor of Maryland. In 1775 he nominated George Washington to be commander in chief of the Continental Army. In 1791 Washington appointed Johnson head of the Commission of Planning for the Federal City. That same year Washington also appointed Johnson associate justice of the United States Supreme Court, and in 1795 he tried to name him secretary of state. (Johnson declined.) Washington and Johnson were born in the same year (1732) and were longtime friends who shared common visions for the new republic and development of the Potomac Valley.

The base of Sugarloaf Mountain was the site of one of several Johnson family iron furnaces, operating from 1787 through the early 1800s. The stream that provided waterpower for the furnace, located within today's Monocacy Natural Resources Management Area, has been known as Furnace Branch ever since. The Johnson family—including brothers Benjamin, Thomas, James, Baker, and Roger—came to Frederick County from Calvert County, Maryland. Several of their eighteenth- and early-nineteenth-century family homes ringing Sugarloaf Mountain have survived to the present day. Construction of Rock Hall Manor, southwest of Sugarloaf near the confluence of Furnace Branch and the Monocacy, was begun by Roger Johnson, a major in the Revolutionary War and active manager of the family businesses.

The Johnson lands at the base of Sugarloaf comprised a bustling industrial center employing large numbers of workers, including an estimated thirty to forty slaves. Charcoal made by local colliers from area trees, limestone, and iron ore (some local but mainly from nearby Point of Rocks) went into the cold-blast furnace process, turning out pig iron that was either sold or, as historians have speculated, carried down a series of trails to Bennett Creek, where the Johnson brothers operated Bloomsbury Forge. Here the pig iron would have been transformed to wrought iron.

The process of turning wood to charcoal (a necessity prior to the use of coal) stripped the area of trees, including large native chestnuts. Some historians speculate that a furnace such as the Johnsons' at the base of Sugarloaf could have required up to an acre of trees per day. In 1786 the Johnsons petitioned the government to obtain formerly Tory woodlots on Sugarloaf to fuel their industries, but they were denied the requested land. However, they were able to run the furnace on their considerable land holdings for many years.

The charcoal-making process involved clearing a flat hearth up to thirty or forty feet in diameter, then stacking wood in a pyramidal structure around a central wooden triangular chimney, which was filled with kindling and fired with hot coals. Prior to being lit, the structure was covered with fallen leaves and then a thick layer of dust to prevent an all-out fire. Colliers tended the charcoal pit for ten days to two weeks, working several pits at a time and making sure the fires burned at the low smoldering rate necessary to create charcoal. Tending the pits was tricky work, and colliers were at the mercy of wind and rain, which could alter the rate of burn and derail the process.

According to *American Charcoal Making:* "When the pit was burning evenly and well, a characteristic blue smoke puffed from the vents at lazy intervals, giving off a pitch tar odor. . . . White smoke was an indication of a poorly charring pit and usually resulted from rapid burning due to too much draft or to the use of old dry wood. Heavy winds caused the pit to burn unevenly, and rains often made it become too hot. When a pit crackled and sputtered it was a certain indication that dry chestnut wood was being employed."[8]

Forest depletion may have contributed to the closing of the Johnson furnace during the early 1800s. Even after that time colliers continued to work their charcoal hearths on the mountain. A Sugarloaf collier family and their teepee-like dwelling were recorded in a watercolor by the eminent architect Benjamin Henry Latrobe, who visited the mountain in the early part of the nineteenth century. Observant visitors to Sugarloaf today will notice the large circular indentations in the earth that pockmark the mountain and are the ruins of these early charcoal hearths.

The Johnsons also quarried the Sugarloaf area for quartzite, and they operated lime kilns, a woolen factory, a grist mill, and a distillery on their extensive holdings. Rock Hall Manor, considered a fine example of federal-style residential architecture, was built by Roger Johnson beginning in 1812. It passed into the hands of his son Joseph, who sold it to the Belt family in the 1830s.[9]

Quarrying for the Monocacy Aqueduct on the Johnson Lands

Claims have been made that the Sugarloaf area was the site of the first primitive railroad. Robert Kapsch, National Park Service senior scholar in historic architecture and historic engineering and an authority on the Monocacy Aqueduct, disputes the oft-held claim of this early railroad's status as the first of its kind, but not the existence or importance of the Sugarloaf railroad itself. Sugarloaf's railroad transported quartzite on horse-drawn platforms along wooden tracks from the mountain base to the mouth of the Monocacy, where the aqueduct was constructed and remains to this day.

Collier and family on the Sugarloaf Mountain, Benjamin Henry Latrobe, 1816. (Courtesy of the Maryland Historical Society, Baltimore)

This horse-powered railroad was an essential cog in the revised version of George Washington's earlier dream of commerce on the Potomac: the C&O Canal. The canal operated from the mid-1800s through the early part of the twentieth century. In more recent times it has been preserved as a National Historical Park. Thanks largely to the efforts of Supreme Court justice William O. Douglas, the C&O Canal has been preserved as "one of the premier natural areas on the East Coast," as Kapsch described it.[10]

The Monocacy Aqueduct, which spans the Monocacy a few miles southwest of Sugarloaf, was constructed between 1829 and 1833. The aqueduct, considered one of the finest masonry structures of its era, is the longest of eleven C&O Canal aqueducts. Several dozen stone masons traveled from the British Isles to build the 516-foot structure. The hard, erosion-resistant quartzite that has held Sugarloaf aloft above the surrounding countryside for the past few million years has stood the aqueduct in good stead during floods, although Hurricane Agnes took a major toll on the structure in 1972, followed by additional damage from the flood of 1985 and those of 1996. In 1998 First Lady Hillary Rodham Clinton and a contingent of dignitaries visited the aqueduct and announced that it had been placed on a National Trust for Historic Preservation list of the country's eleven most endangered historic places. Since then, through the efforts of the Chesapeake & Ohio Canal Association and other organizations and individuals, several million dollars has been allocated for the National Park Service to renovate the aqueduct, facilitating the removal of the unsightly steel girders that have been a stabilizing necessity in recent years.

Sugarloaf's quarries also contributed some of the stone for the Monocacy Viaduct, originally constructed in 1869–73 for the Metropolitan Branch of the B&O Railroad. The viaduct, an approximately seven-hundred-foot railroad bridge on masonry piers located about two thousand feet upriver from the aqueduct, was the longest and most expensive original structure built on the Metropolitan Branch line. By the time of its construction, Rock Hall and the Sugarloaf quarries had passed into the hands of the Belt family, who owned the manor house and lands for many years.

The Metropolitan Branch, when it opened in 1873, created new markets for Sugarloaf-area farmers. According to *Circling Historic Landscapes:* "A large dairy industry grew along the right-of-way around Dickerson, where farmers were soon hauling five gallon cans of cream to the 6 A.M. 'milk train' for Washington."[11]

Today the quarries and the Roger Johnson home are owned by the state of Maryland and administered under the Department of Natural Resources. The Johnson house was renovated in recent years by curators Jon and Sally Mullen. The quarry and lime kiln ruins lie within the boundaries of the twenty-one-hundred-acre Monocacy Natural Resources Management Area (described on p. 65). What historians believe to be the earthen outlines of the primitive railroad can still be seen in a few places. All that remains of the Johnson furnace is a slag heap along Furnace Branch, just upstream from the confluence with the Monocacy. The privately owned Johnson family home between Bennett Creek and Peters Road, long known as Old Forge Farm, marks the spot of Bloomsbury Forge.

Roger Johnson, who had become the prime manager of the Sugarloaf enterprises on and around the mountain before the turn of the nineteenth century, and who was the second-largest taxpayer in Frederick County, soon went into serious debt. The Bank of the United

Monocacy Aqueduct during the Civil War. ("Aqueduct of the Chesapeake and Ohio Canal, at the mouth of the Monocacy—present position of General Banks's Army," Harper's Weekly, September 14, 1861, Library of Congress Collection)

States foreclosed on many of his holdings and acquired much of the Sugarloaf area, dividing the mountain into fifty or so woodlots that were resold during the 1800s. While most were bought up by local residents, the well-known philanthropist William Corcoran purchased the summit of the mountain. The summit was to play a prominent role during the Civil War.

The Amelung Glassworks

The Johnson brothers were not the only early industrialists to exploit the plentiful resources of the Sugarloaf Mountain region. In 1784 Bennett Creek, near the current-day Park Mills settlement, became the site of what Fritz Gutheim called "the most significant episode in the history of early American glass."[12] John Frederick Amelung, his family, and an entourage of skilled glassworkers—as well as teachers, physicians, butchers, bakers, blacksmiths, and shoemakers (in short, all the essential personnel for a self-contained community devoted to glassmaking)—immigrated from Bremen, Germany, and founded the colony of New Bremen on land that had been part of the large and renowned Carrollton Manor. Amelung built glass factories, homes for members of his New Bremen community, and a twenty-two-room mansion called Mountvina, which survives to this day. He established a school teaching English, German, French, writing, ciphering, and music—and an orchestra. According to Gutheim: "The employees at the glassworks were organized into a full orchestra, and performed not only for balls, but on every ceremonial occasion. A half century afterward, in the spacious attic of Mountvina, a bored little girl accompanied by her mother on a visit, found four gold harps."[13]

Amelung's glass, which today is prized by collectors and has been displayed in the Metropolitan Museum of Art in New York City, included practical items such as windows and mirrors, jelly glasses, and bottles. But according to Gutheim, "[T]he finest were the beautifully clear, slightly smoke-toned presentation pieces he seems to have made for the express purpose of winning friends for the new enterprise." Amelung presented George Washington with a pair of flint glass goblets and his neighbor Baker Johnson with "a set of case bottles, duly inscribed and dated in a wreath of laurels ornamented by the traditional motif of two doves."[14]

Amelung struggled to keep his enterprise afloat, competing with cheaply priced foreign-made glass and petitioning both the state of Maryland and the U.S. Congress for assistance in the form of loans and tariffs. He received loans from Maryland but was less successful with Congress. According to historical research conducted by Ken Perkins: "His appeals to Congress for loans and tariffs marked the first time that Congress debated the constitutional question of whether the government could support private business."[15]

Perkins noted that Amelung "suffered a disastrous fire in 1790 and declared bankruptcy in 1795. He died a broken man in 1798."[16] His workers and glassworks machinery, however, went on contributing to the young republic's burgeoning glass industry. Thomas Johnson purchased some of the Amelung machinery and opened the Aetna glassworks on Bush Creek and another glassworks on Tuscarora Creek. According to Gutheim, Amelung workers manned the plants and traveled to other parts of the young nation to work in glass manufacturing: "A foreman named Kolenberg bought Amelung's second glass house on Bear Branch, and operated it for years."[17]

The vision of John Frederick Amelung left a decided legacy for a new nation. Around 1810 the Fleecy Dale Woolen Factory began operations near the site of Amelung's former glassworks. Fleecy Dale was in business for several decades, but is not associated with any surviving structure.

The Civil War

Sugarloaf stood at the heart of Civil War troop movements, Union and Confederate encampments, and minor skirmishes. The Battle of Ball's Bluff and the Battle of Monocacy took place nearby, and Sugarloaf played an important role in the prelude to the catastrophic Battle of Antietam. In the shadow of Sugarloaf Mountain many families were divided by Northern and Southern sympathies. Although Maryland stayed in the Union, many men from Montgomery and Frederick Counties crossed the Potomac to join up with Confederate fighting forces. Maryland was a slave state, and a number of local

families were slave owners. The Underground Railroad also was an
active force in the region, helping escaped slaves travel to freedom
in Canada.

Because of its strategic location and unimpeded view, Sugarloaf's
summit (then owned by William Corcoran) became a signal station
for the Union cause and served as a field training center for the Signal Corps. Signals were relayed back and forth across the countryside
from the mountain ridges to the west and on to Poolesville and Washington through the use of signal flags, flares, and telegraph. According to legendary Frederick-area writer Folger McKinsey (known by
the pen name "The Bentztown Bard"):

> What Mr. Corcoran's dream was for the summit of Sugar Loaf Mountain,
> is not known. But that summit has doubtless set many a man dreaming.
> . . . [I]n the early 1860's, men were not dreaming about the summit of
> Sugar Loaf Mountain. They were dreaming on it—under their white can-
> vas tents. They had built a high log tower.
>
> From its top, from dawn to dusk men looked out through their glasses
> over that beautiful Virginia country, across the river—enemy country. The
> Federal army had found Sugar Loaf Mountain its most important observa-
> tion point anywhere near the Federal capital. The Signal Service lived
> there, winter and summer. They looked, and what they saw they wigwaged
> to other stations miles away.[18]

A 1932 article by Helen Urner Price in the Washington, D.C., *Sunday Star* contained another vivid account of the Civil War Signal
Corps on Sugarloaf:

> No other part of the Civil War's military services caused as much curiosity
> and interest as did the Signal Corps. Their mystic messages were charged
> with thrilling importance. In every campaign their flags flaunted defiantly
> at the front, sending warnings of danger, speeding orders of advance or ac-
> knowledging defeat. The extreme danger of the work is shown by the fact
> that the killed of the Signal Corps were 150 per cent greater than the usual
> ratio of the fatally wounded.
>
> The majority of the signal messages sent from the Sugar Loaf were by
> means of flags, torches or lights in combinations of three separate motions.

The flag (or torch) was first held upright; "one" was indicated by waving the flag to the left and returning it from the ground to the upright position; "two" by a similar motion to the right and "three" by a dip to the front. Where a letter was composed of several figures the motions were made quickly without pause. Letters were separated by a brief pause and words or sentences were indicated by dip motions to the front.[19]

On a day in early September 1862, a Lieutenant Miner was in command of the Sugarloaf signal station. What he saw from the summit that day was the prelude to what still stands as the bloodiest single day in American history: the Battle of Antietam. Miner signaled news of his observations on toward the capital, where McClellan's forces were gathering: Lee's army was crossing the Potomac into Maryland at White's Ford (about a mile downriver from the present-day Dickerson Conservation Park).

This historic crossing, which took several days, is one of the most poignant episodes of the Civil War. "Dirty, ragged and half starved, the Marylanders in the Confederate Army tossed their hats in the air and wept with joy when they reached the shores of home," Price wrote. "Some of them knelt and kissed the sod."[20]

Sugarloaf Mountain during the Civil War. ("Topographical Camp at Sugar-Loaf Mountain," Harper's New Monthly Magazine, September 1866, Library of Congress Collection)

Stephen W. Sears described the scene in his book *Landscape Turned Red: The Battle of Antietam:*

> On Thursday, September 4, advance elements of the Army of Northern Virginia pushed on to White's Ford on the Potomac and began crossing into Maryland, an operation that continued through the weekend. There was a universal sense that here was a historic moment. Men long remembered the glowing pastoral scene. The Potomac, shallow and a half mile wide, flowed gently under the golden autumn sun past richly wooded green banks. The sunrise, Sergeant Shinn wrote in his diary, "caused the rippled surface to sparkle with the brilliancy of a sea of silver studded with diamonds set in dancing beds of burnished gold. . . . The scene was one of grand & magnificent interest." Bands played "Maryland, My Maryland," and the men were cheerful, splashing through the waist-deep water, yipping the Rebel yell. The only thing Lieutenant William Johnson, of the 2nd South Carolina, found wrong with the crossing was that it was too brief. "We needed a good washing of our bodies," he wrote, "but wading in the water did us no good in that direction."
>
> Even Stonewall Jackson unbent, sitting his horse in the middle of the river and tipping his battered forage cap to the cheers of his men.[21]

On the Maryland side of the river, "local citizens heard the music and came to enjoy the entertainment," wrote Sugarloaf-country resident Margaret Marshall Coleman in her book *Montgomery County: A Pictorial History:*

> Meanwhile, someone raided a barge on the C&O Canal and came away with watermelons for everyone. . . .
>
> For three days the lines of troops came, as more than thirty thousand men crossed the river into Maryland. By nightfall of September 8, the last of the barefoot infantrymen sloshed onto the miry bank and lowered his rifle and bedroll from over his head.
>
> Two of the officers, Colonel White and his commander, General Stonewall Jackson, went to Dickerson for dinner, followed by their men. White's mother-in-law, Mary Elizabeth Trundle Gott, collected her friends and prepared ham, fried chicken, potatoes, corn, squash, and blackberry pie for the sudden but welcome guests.[22]

The Confederate troops swarmed into Montgomery and Frederick Counties on a wave of high optimism, banking on—and clearly encountering at least some—local support. During the second week in September, J. E. B. Stuart attended a ball in Urbana, although military action called him away from the dance floor. The celebratory spirit of the crossing would not last. On September 17, many of those who had joyfully splashed through the Potomac on a warm late-summer day lay dead on the battlefields along Antietam Creek. By the end of that day, 3,654 Confederate and Union soldiers were dead. The wounded, captured, and missing brought the total number of casualties to 22,728.[23] And for the first time ever, many civilians would appreciate the true horrors of war through the uncensored battlefield photographs put on display in Matthew Brady's gallery in New York City.

Soon after the White's Ford crossing, Confederate forces captured the Sugarloaf signal station and held it for several days before it was recaptured by Union forces. Confederate troops tried to destroy the Monocacy Aqueduct without success. During the war at least one makeshift hospital was set up at the base of the mountain in a cottage that still stands. Many Civil War artifacts have been recovered on and near the mountain, including buttons, shells, swords, and bullets. At Rock Hall Manor, occupying troops left bayonet marks where they pried open the cabinets.

The Civil War was kind to one Sugarloaf resident, Ephraim Harris, who is remembered in the names of two rural roads near the mountain base, Mount Ephraim and West Harris, and the fine brick home at their crossroads. Harris, whose farming family had extensive land holdings dating back to the eighteenth century, recognized a business opportunity in the comings and goings associated with the war. He set up a store at the crossroads that did a brisk business during and after the war. The area became known as Mount Ephraim; local lore holds that the name had to do with Ephraim Harris's height.

In 1868 the prolific local builder William T. Hilton constructed the red-brick home for Harris that still bears the name Mount Ephraim. Later it would become the residence of two distinguished men and their families. The first was François F. Darrieulat, President Theodore Roosevelt's fencing master, coach of two U.S. Olympic fencing

teams, and friend of Gordon Strong. His daughter, Jacqueline
Nichols, remembered washing a sibling's diapers in a mountain
stream during childhood stays at Sugarloaf.[24]

Later, Fritz Gutheim, a well-known author who was a key player
in regional preservation, occupied the house with his wife, Mary, better known as Polly, and his son, Nicholas. Fritz was an author of the
Maryland–National Capital Park and Planning Commission's Master
Plan for Historic Preservation in Montgomery County and founder
of Sugarloaf Regional Trails, a conservation-education organization
and producer of books and films. The erudite Fritz drove a blue Volk-
swagen Beetle, wore a baseball cap, and loved to take visitors out
back to Polly's chicken coop, where he would offer them the pleasure of holding a warm egg.

Gordon Strong and Stronghold

By 1900 a badly denuded Sugarloaf was almost as battle-scarred as
the postbellum South. But the era of patchwork woodlots was about
to end. The twentieth century dawned most auspiciously for Sugarloaf Mountain, for it was discov-
ered by a young man with a cohe-
sive vision.

Gordon Strong
(Courtesy of Stronghold, Inc.)

Henry Gordon Strong (known
simply as Gordon Strong)—the
man who would single-handedly
save an unspoiled Sugarloaf for
posterity—was a complex person.
Gordon was the only surviving son
of General Henry Strong, a Scot-
tish immigrant who rose to become president and director of the
Atchison, Topeka & Santa Fe Rail-
way. Henry, an attorney, was in
charge of building the railroad
west from Topeka; earlier, he had
helped build the Chicago, Burlington & Quincy (formerly the Bur-

lington & Missouri) across Iowa. Henry made millions in real estate, primarily in Chicago and Washington, D.C., before his death in 1911.

Gordon Strong was born in Burlington, Iowa, in 1869, one of nine children of Henry and Mary Strong, only four of whom survived childhood. The family moved to Chicago, and by all accounts it was while visiting the family's summer home on Lake Geneva in Wisconsin that Gordon developed his strong love of the outdoors.

Henry Strong sent his son to two of the country's most prestigious schools: Phillips Exeter Academy and Harvard. Gordon Strong also attended the university in Heidelberg, where he fell in love with the rolling landscapes, people, and architecture of the Rhine country. He received two law degrees from the Columbian University Law School (today's George Washington) in Washington, D.C.

The young Gordon Strong served in the military in Cuba during the Spanish-American War (he would become Colonel Strong during World War I when he organized and funded a National Guard regiment). He then worked as a patent attorney and real estate manager in Chicago, managing many of his father's properties and successfully striking out on his own in both Chicago and Washington, D.C.

According to many accounts, it was during the 1890s, while Gordon Strong was on a bicycle trip with a friend near Frederick, that Sugarloaf Mountain first made a strong impression on him. (David F. Webster, executive secretary/treasurer of Stronghold, said that Strong had seen Sugarloaf through the window of a train prior to the bicycle trip.)

In 1903 Gordon Strong bought his first piece of property on Sugarloaf—and he never looked back.[25] By midcentury, at the time of his death, he would own some 2,350 acres of Sugarloaf Mountain real estate. (Stronghold, Inc. has since acquired an additional several hundred acres.) In an effort to keep local woodlot owners in the dark about his grand scheme to buy up the mountain—and to keep prices low—Strong often used straw buyers to intervene. One story tells how Strong dressed as a poor woodcutter to convince William Corcoran to take pity on him and sell him the summit of the mountain. This story cannot be true as told (Corcoran died in 1888), but perhaps Strong used some sort of creative deceit with Corcoran's nephew. A 1904 edition of a Frederick, Maryland, publication called *The Citizen* reported: "Mr. Corcoran . . . conveyed the property to one of his nephews by the name of Jones. Subsequently it has been sold to a man whose name I have been unable to learn."[26] Another article in the Frederick *News-Post* claimed that Corcoran had deeded the summit to his nephew, William T. Jones of Montgomery County, in 1880.

In 1907 Strong retained a Philadelphia architect named Percy Ashe who designed for him a grand, three-winged, fifty-four-room Georgian manor. The home, begun in 1912, served as a part-time residence for Gordon and his wife, Louise Strong, and from 1936 on it was their permanent home. Louise was Gordon's secretary and his second wife. In her, Strong gained a life partner who shared his love for Sugarloaf.

The home, once called Southwoodside and today referred to simply as the Strong Mansion, has walls constructed of reinforced concrete with a stuccoed and cut-stone exterior. The mansion was never completed as designed, but artwork survives that documents the grandeur (some might say grandiosity) of its conception. Whether it was financial realities or, as many believe, Louise's common sense that intervened, only the western third of the mansion was constructed.

The original design for the Strong Mansion. Only the western third was completed. (Courtesy of Stronghold, Inc.)

The Strong Mansion today

Gordon Strong built a gravel road up the mountain during the 1920s and carved out several scenic viewpoints along the way. Stone steps were created to take hikers—many of them in rather formal attire—to the summit. Stone walls and accents were added; lavish gardens, ponds, and watercourses were created or planned; and several other homes and two schools were built on the grounds. Visitors were welcomed on weekends, and people began to come to witness the beauty that had so captivated Strong. Writers who were among the first to describe Gordon Strong's Sugarloaf oozed hyperbole. Helen Urner Price's story for the Washington, D.C., *Sunday Star,* dated July 17, 1932, ran under the title, "Weird Mountain Beauty in New Park—Lordly Sugar Loaf, a Strange Formation of Peaks, Situated Above the Potomac Valley in Maryland, Where Signals of War Once Flared, Lures Travelers to Its Paths of Scenic Splendor—A Delightful Motor Trip From Washington."

Here is a sampling of Price's observations about the mountain's charms and Gordon Strong's innovations:

Standing majestically on the side of the mountain that overlooks the Potomac Valley, the white walls of a stately house can be seen for miles around. This mansion, of classic Georgian simplicity, is the Summer home of Mr. and Mrs. Strong. From the house to the lagoon at the edge of the grounds slope the terraces of an Italian garden, an entrancing place of white balustrades, sparkling fountains and shimmering pools.

Immediately upon entering the grounds one feels the charm of the Sugar Loaf. Here is the cool tranquility of a great forest. In the Springtime the flowers of laurel and dogwood blossom in pink and white profusion. Big bushes of bridal wreath trail their snowy strands. Golden forsythia, purple rhododendrons, salmon-colored azalea bloom exotically among the trees.

In a corner of the park a water garden with lagoons and flowery islands is being constructed.

Traveling through the forest one emerges suddenly upon an Elysian spot in the wilderness. A semi-circular seat, made of native rose-tinted stone and raised upon a circular platform of the same delicately-colored blocks, forms a regal dais that overlooks, as it were, the world.

Steps hewn out of the rock form a stairway to the summit. Rain water caught in tarpaulin-covered barrels was used to mix the concrete. Out of reach of machinery and modern contrivances, the construction of this mountain stairway was a remarkable achievement.

Right up to the loftiest point go the steps. There one comes upon stark splendor. Towering boulders, gaunt, overhanging cliffs, trees silhouetted against the clouds, beauty wild, superb, terrifying.

Unfolding on every side are glorious panoramas. Beyond the far-flung Maryland fields soar the Catoctin heights. Bursting through the mountain gateway at Point of Rocks the Potomac River swirls in a silvery stream, while to the south, stretching out in calm loveliness, the Valley of the Potomac meets the Shenandoah and Blue Ridge. Rolling away to the east are fields and billowing spurs.

On a clear day one can see the dome of the Capitol.[27]

A Sugarloaf visitor's experience today in springtime is apt to be remarkably similar to the writer's of seventy years ago. The flowering trees and shrubs—both native and cultivated—still thrive and dazzle the eye. The semicircular seat at Gordon Strong's "First View" (dubbed "Trustees' Circle" in later years in honor of the members of the Stronghold board who held their first meeting there) still invites contemplation. And the stone steps to the summit and its glorious panoramas remain intact. Some of the more lavish ponds and lagoons are no longer extant, but the landscaping around Sugarloaf still holds much of the grandeur of Gordon and Louise's day. In recent years, Stronghold has created a new memorial garden in honor of Gordon Strong and two early Stronghold trustees using the original stone accents surrounding what was once a pool. The Strong Memorial Garden is downhill from the Strong Mansion and can be reached through a spruce-lined lane from the White Trail (see chapter 3).

Gordon Strong began keeping records of his visitors. In 1926 he recorded 788, and by 1941, 31,000.[28] At present, Stronghold estimates that nearly a quarter-million people visit the mountain annually, and the Strong Mansion is rented for weddings and special parties. But had Gordon Strong yielded to two of the twentieth century's most formidable personalities, visitors today might not be coming to Sugarloaf at all, or they might be coming for an experience radically different from the tranquil one that still awaits.

"The Automobile Objective"

The family automobile was a novelty, and Gordon Strong wanted to use the car to create a thrilling experience for his visitors. In 1924 he engaged the renowned architect Frank Lloyd Wright to execute a dramatic plan for Sugarloaf's summit.

In a letter dated September 22, 1924, Strong outlined his vision for Wright. He wanted to build a structure on the summit that would accommodate two hundred to five hundred cars within the building itself, with storage sheds for a thousand more. The idea was for the summit to "serve as an objective [the project has often been called 'the Automobile Objective'] for short motor trips on the part of residents of the vicinity, particularly of Washington and Baltimore." Daytime and evening dining would be provided, along with indoor and outdoor dancing with live music and limited lodging, but most

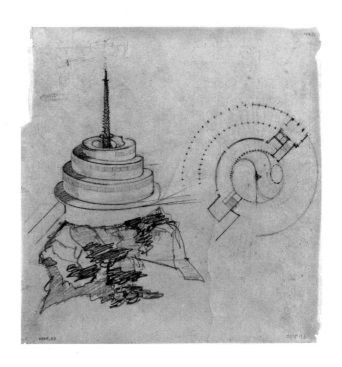

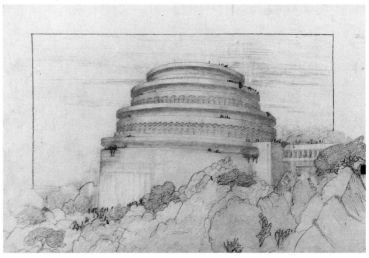

Frank Lloyd Wright drawings of Sugarloaf "Automobile Objective." (Copyright 1996, 2002, The Frank Lloyd Wright Foundation, Scottsdale, Arizona)

essential would be the creation of "open terraces" and "covered galleries" to dramatize the view. Strong wanted his innovation to be "striking, impressive, so that everyone hearing of the place will want to come once . . . beautiful, satisfying, so that those coming will want to come again . . . enduring, so that the structure will constitute a permanent and creditable monument, instead of proving a merely transitory novelty."[29]

During the ensuing year, Wright drafted his plans for the summit of Sugarloaf. He designed a dramatic spiral auto ramp around the outside of a large circular structure and added a planetarium and theater for good measure. Written correspondence between the architect and Gordon Strong was, for the most part, warm and cordial. However, tensions between the two are evident. There was confusion about the space available on the summit, and at one point Wright quipped: "The way that mountain swells and shrinks! It leaves me quite dizzy."[30]

The Strongs were invited to spend Thanksgiving of 1924 at Taliesin, Wright's Wisconsin home. Gordon Strong declined the invitation, with cordial thanks and the explanation that "the time has come when I count moments and cut out everything that consumes them—that is, everything but the work I have to do and which has to be done."[31] Wright was disappointed and Strong subsequently defensive. The written correspondence between the two contains no apparent prelude, however, to the sudden and complete rejection of Wright's plan contained in a letter dated October 14, 1925.

In the letter, Strong objected to the plan to build the spiral auto ramp on the exterior of the structure, saying he'd prefer that people be able to sit on outdoor terraces "unobstructed by automobiles." To Wright, an architect esteemed for sensitivity to his design sites, the following assessment by Strong must have been galling: "Your proposed 'automobile observatory' impresses me as just that. As a structure of complete unity and independence, without any relation to its surroundings."

In his zeal to prove Wright unoriginal, Gordon Strong went all the way back to biblical architecture. "I must admit," he wrote, "that the exterior ramps are archeologically right. They prove overwhelmingly your close adherence to tradition. In devising the latest type of struc-

ture, you have gone straight back to the earliest." He then wrote that
he was enclosing a picture of the Tower of Babel. The letter is signed,
"In spite of which, I remain Very cordially yours, Gordon Strong."[32]
Within days, Wright wrote back. In response to Strong's compar-
ison of the Sugarloaf design to the Tower of Babel, the architect
stated: "But why the ponderous precedents and omit the law of grav-
itation in your category? And the fact that every carpenter that drives
a screw proves me standardized and unoriginal. Every spiral spring
shows me up. I have found it hard to look a snail in the face since I
stole the idea of his house—from his back." Wright added: "I am
sorry you fail to see how the natural snail-crown of the great
couchant lion,—is grown up from his mountain head, the very quality of its movement, rising and adapting itself to the uninterrupted
movement of people sitting comfortably in their own cars in a novel
circumstance with the whole landscape revolving about them, as exposed to view as though they were in an aeroplane."[33]

As to why Strong decided against Wright's design, one local story
credits Louise Strong. In 1996 a traveling exhibit featuring five Frank
Lloyd Wright projects that were never built was held at the Library
of Congress. The Sugarloaf Automobile Objective was one of the
five projects portrayed through drawings, three-dimensional models,
and written text. At the time of the exhibit, Washington Post architectural critic Benjamin Forgey weighed in on Wright's conception
for Sugarloaf. Wrote Forgey: "Designed for the very top of our local
mountain, the 'automobile objective' is the most dramatic of the
projects. . . . Strong lost his nerve, so it didn't get built. This is just as
well. Given the tremendous increase in size, power and number of
cars, the building would have been a ponderous curiosity. Still, it was
a powerfully poetic conception, celebrating the unity of landscape
and architecture—the building seems literally an extension of the
mountain."[34]

Wright later adapted his spiral design for the Guggenheim Museum in New York City and some lesser known projects, while
Strong's plans for Sugarloaf Mountain would soon be tested again.

Franklin Delano Roosevelt and Sugarloaf Mountain

Franklin Delano Roosevelt visited Sugarloaf several times during his presidency. According to David F. Webster, Roosevelt especially enjoyed being driven up the mountain, where he could look out toward  the west over the Frederick (or Monocacy) Valley. According to many accounts, Roosevelt wished to obtain the mountain as a White House retreat, but Gordon Strong refused to part with it, suggesting that the president look toward the Catoctins and the present-day Camp David (formerly Shangri-La). Of this, Webster is quoted as saying: "Strong never once considered selling his mountain, but he was much too diplomatic to refuse the president outright."[35]

In an unpublished paper about Gordon Strong and Sugarloaf, Fritz Gutheim described how Harold L. Ickes, Roosevelt's secretary of the interior, attempted to obtain Sugarloaf as a White House retreat. (Ickes was the father of another Harold Ickes, who served in President Clinton's White House.)

"Ickes called on Strong," wrote Gutheim. "The two Chicagoans faced each other . . . [Ickes] knew Gordon Strong would fight to the finish for his mountain home, and must have been pleased when Strong suggested another location a few miles north in the Catoctins."[36]

Present-day visitors who enjoy Sugarloaf's trails are probably just as glad that the mountain never became a White House retreat. Still, it's nice to think of the president enjoying some serene moments picnicking on Sugarloaf, away from the challenges of national office. Stronghold has cleared the view to the west that Roosevelt enjoyed and named it "the Roosevelt View." You can enjoy it yourself from the West View parking lot and picnic area.

Gordon Strong and Education

When Henry Strong died in 1911 he left his son a trust fund to be used for the purpose of education. Gordon Strong built two schools at the mountain—one for white children and one for black. (Segregation remained the rule throughout much of America during the early twentieth century.)

On or around 1912 Strong built and opened the Comstock School on Mount Ephraim Road for local black children, naming it for his grandmother Mercy Comstock. The one-story, yellow-sided school still stands, serving as an occasional meeting place for the surrounding Mount Ephraim community. Strong maintained the school for Frederick County, augmenting the teacher's monthly salary and extending the school year from April 15 to May 31 to correspond with the calendar of local white schools.

The small schoolhouse served grades one through seven, with the first-graders up front and the desks and chairs getting larger toward the back as the children were seated according to grade level. The lone teacher started with the youngest children and worked her way to the back of the classroom, which was heated by a wood stove on cold days. Paul Wilson, a longtime Mount Ephraim community member, attended the school from the age of six in 1922 to graduation in 1930. In his words: "The children loved to go to school and it was the best school in the county."[37]

The Halstead School (recently moved to the right side of the road up Sugarloaf near the mountain base) served the white community, both local children and fourteen boys whom Gordon and Louise Strong, who never had children of their own, brought to live with them at the mansion over the years. Two of those children, Donald and John McCormack, would be active trustees and officers of Stronghold for many years. Current family members of John McCormack (including daughters Marion M. Webster and Joan M. Rice and son-in-law David F. Webster) serve on the Stronghold board.

The Halstead School (top) and Comstock School (bottom)

Strong's Legacy

In 1936 Gordon and Louise Strong made Sugarloaf their permanent home. From that time on, Gordon Strong thought long and deeply about the future of his beloved mountain. In his will, which he finalized in 1943, he included an elaborate plan specifically preserving the mountain for the benefit and enjoyment of future generations. In 1946, eight years before his death, Strong recorded his charter for Sugarloaf Mountain, setting the land aside for visitor enjoyment, to be administered by the private, nonprofit Stronghold corporation. Later, a trust fund was established to be administered by Riggs Bank, where the McCormack brothers served as officers. Initially, 250 acres and the road up the mountain were leased to Stronghold, with ten thousand dollars a year allocated for operation.[38] Upon Strong's death the remaining acreage, the mansion, and other dwelling places would be owned and operated by Stronghold.

The Certificate of Incorporation of Stronghold, Incorporated, recorded by the state of Maryland on April 9, 1946, and signed by Gordon Strong, Louise Strong, and Donald McCormack, described the purpose of Stronghold: "To acquire land by lease, purchase, gift and/or devise; to develop such land with roads and other appropriate forms of landscape and/or architectural treatment; to offer to visitors for their enjoyment and education, access to such land so developed; to take such other steps as shall appear desirable and compatible, toward public enjoyment of and education in out-of-door beauty as one of the great sources of human happiness; and to engage in such incidental activities as promote and are compatible with the foregoing purpose."[39]

Following Gordon Strong's death, and in accordance with his instructions, the charter of Stronghold, Inc. was amended and revised to specifically incorporate and make permanent the directives in his will. In the revised charter, the passage quoted above was restated and strengthened, with the reference to "visitors" changed to "the public" and the last line expanded to read: "and to engage in such incidental activities as promote and are compatible with the foregoing purposes all with the aim of promoting the physical and mental development of the greatest natural resource of this nation, its people."[40]

Gordon Strong made eloquent statements about the importance of natural beauty in related writings, some of which are quoted in the introduction to this book. He especially believed in the transformational quality of views, such as the ones from the summit and shoulders of Sugarloaf.

Strong considered handing his park over to the federal or state government, but decided against it, opting for a private nonprofit corporation operating under his instructions for management. Stronghold's present-day caretakers—the board of trustees, currently made up of ten members, and a small administrative and maintenance staff augmented by volunteers—maintain Sugarloaf's wild areas and care for the gardens and grounds of the Strong Mansion and other dwellings and cultivated areas.

What sort of man was Gordon Strong? His industriousness and generosity were legendary. People who knew him well or were acquaintances have commented on his erudition, his quick wit, and also his reserved and gentlemanly manner, sometimes characterized as aloofness.

In Fritz Gutheim's words: "Gordon Strong was a tall, thin man— perhaps six feet three. He had what is sometimes called a military bearing. He was much given to whimsy in both the spoken and written forms. This took the form of nicknames, literary and historical references, applications of military, medical and other specialized terms. . . . Perhaps the personal characteristic I would describe . . . is Strong's kindness. He was a good employer."[41]

Strong took pride and pleasure in watching his visitors enjoy the splendors of Sugarloaf Mountain. Gutheim wrote: "[H]e would post himself at the stone stair leading to the very top of the mountain hoping to learn from visitor comments the answer to his perpetual question, 'now that we have [this] tract of land 35 miles from the nation's capital, what is the best thing we can do with it?'"[42]

Strong's own answer to that question is the combination of wild and cultivated beauty greeting every Sugarloaf visitor today. By acquiring and preserving a mountain of uncommon beauty, Strong assured his legacy. Long before the first Earth Day in 1970, Gordon Strong recognized the importance of natural beauty as a central experience of human life.

Sugarloaf Mountain: A National Natural Landmark

On June 19, 1969, then Secretary of the Interior Walter J. Hickel came to the mountain and unveiled a bronze plaque designating Sugarloaf a "Registered Natural Landmark." The plaque is displayed on a large rock on the western side of the parking lot at the mountain base. Secretary Hickel extolled the foresight of Gordon Strong and proclaimed: "Parks like this will help solve some of the problems of the cities by giving the public a chance to see the countryside in all its natural beauty."[43]

Sugarloaf Mountain is also recognized as "an area of Critical State Concern by Maryland for its unique topographic features and as an important breeding area for many species of wildlife," according to the Maryland Environmental Trust.[44]

Stronghold Activities Today

The Program to Revive the American Chestnut

In 1969 a symposium on the fate of the American chestnut was held at the Strong Mansion, and during the ensuing years scientists have conducted research at the mountain aimed at developing a chestnut tree that can survive the chestnut blight. Prior to 1900 the American chestnut *(Castanea dentata)* was a dominant tree of eastern forests, including those of the Sugarloaf region. The tree provided both the famous chestnut fruit and valuable lumber. Early settlers used the wood to build homes and furniture. As mentioned in chapter 2, many Sugarloaf trees were felled to fuel charcoal furnaces and other industries of the eighteenth and nineteenth centuries.

But no woodcutter could approximate the kind of damage that was done when a fungus *(Endothia parasitica)* arrived in the United States early in the twentieth century, probably on seedlings of imported Japanese or Chinese chestnuts. Within a few decades the giant chestnut forests were gone. However, scientists working at Sugarloaf and elsewhere are testing trees grown from irradiated seeds. The trees that are part of this research are planted near the mountain base. Scientists hope that through experimentation they will eventually develop a strain that can withstand the blight, which kills the tree from the roots up.

You may find chestnut saplings growing along the trails; these are the shoots the living roots keep sending up, only to be knocked back down by the blight. Occasionally an American chestnut will grow large and strong enough to produce fruit, but whether the chestnut giants will ever return to the forests is unknown.

Stronghold's Forestry Demonstration Program

During the 1990s Stronghold established a forestry demonstration area along Mount Ephraim Road on the west side of Sugarloaf. The Stronghold board approved and donated more than a hundred acres for the demonstration area, designed by Mike Kay, Frederick project forester for the Maryland Department of Natural Resources Forestry Programs. The program, which demonstrates several types of forestry practices, is used as both a study and a demonstration area for specific logging operations, including clear-cut, seed tree, shelter wood, group selection, and single tree selection. In 2000, for example, a group of fifteen foresters from the Guizhou Province of China visited Sugarloaf to learn about timber harvesting practices that do not cause undue erosion. According to Stronghold: "The Maryland Forest Service informed the group of different recommendations for planning and implementing erosion and sediment control practices and the results of a scientific study of water quality during and after logging."[45]

Nature Study at Sugarloaf

Many local naturalists study and record the native plant and animal populations for which Sugarloaf is a critical source of unspoiled habitat. During spring migration and seasonal census-taking, birders flock to the mountain's trails and overlooks.

Yellow school buses frequently switchback up the mountain road carrying groups of youngsters on field trips from schools throughout the Maryland/Virginia/D.C. area. According to the *Sugarloaf Mountain Newsletter:* "Every year 3200 Frederick County fifth grade students, along with 300 parents and 50 teachers, incorporate Sugarloaf Mountain into their Geology Program. The program is headed by Eddie Main, Director of Frederick County Outdoor Education. They learn about the early history of the mountain, geology and Gordon Strong."[46] Stronghold office manager Susan Dunn said some of the parents now accompanying fifth-graders took part in the program when they were schoolchildren themselves.

The most important environmental education that goes on at Sugarloaf is undoubtedly the unstructured kind. Families come to Sugarloaf for leisurely strolls and picnics during which children discover the wonders of this natural setting as they scramble over the rocks and explore the trails at an unhurried pace. According to Neal Fitzpatrick, executive director of the Audubon Naturalist Society in Chevy Chase, Maryland, the Sugarloaf area provides a unique and essential mosaic of woodland, wetland, and farmland habitats. As encroaching suburbs creep ever closer, these habitats grow more precious.

3 Sugarloaf's Trail System

Stronghold, Inc. maintains a trail system for hiking that is kept in good condition by staff and volunteers. Stronghold encourages volunteer trail maintenance, and many schools and groups participate. (See p. 8 for address and phone numbers.) All major trails are marked with colored blazes, and the trails intersect in ways that make it easy to vary routes and to plan circuit hikes. Trails can be accessed from East View, West View, and the base of the mountain. The Blue Trail and the Yellow Trail also cross Mount Ephraim Road. The Yellow Trail, a seven-mile loop around the lower slopes of the mountain, can be used by horseback riders and (during late spring, summer, and early fall weekdays only) mountain bikers. Individual trail descriptions begin on page 51.

You may pick up a trail map at East View, West View, or at the wooden building on the left just beyond the gated entrance to the road up the mountain. Stronghold's official hiking map identifies each trail by the color of the blazes (painted rectangles or circles) you will see on trees when you are hiking. Rectangular blazes mark hiking trails, and circular blazes denote the multiuse Yellow Trail. When trails overlap you will find alternating blazes for each. A double blaze (two painted rectangles or circles on a single tree) means a sharp turn or a junction, and diamond-shaped blazes designate spur trails. For instance, two separate spur trails, marked with white diamonds, connect the White Trail with East View and Potomac Overlook.

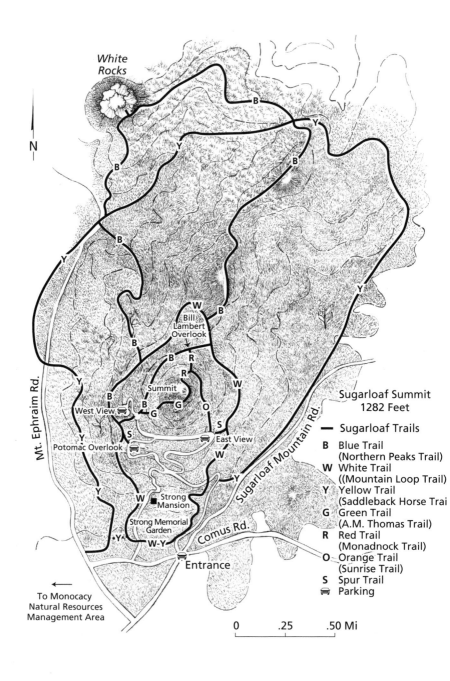

White
Rocks

N

Bill
Lambert
Overlook

W

B

Summit

B

R

R

G

G

O

W

West View

B

S

Potomac Overlook

S

East View

Y

W

Mt. Ephraim Rd.

W

Strong
Mansion

Strong Memorial
Garden

W-Y

Comus Rd.

Sugarloaf Mountain Rd.

Entrance

To Monocacy
Natural Resources
Management Area

Sugarloaf Summit
1282 Feet

— Sugarloaf Trails

B   Blue Trail
    (Northern Peaks Trail)
W   White Trail
    ((Mountain Loop Trail)
Y   Yellow Trail
    (Saddleback Horse Trai
G   Green Trail
    (A.M. Thomas Trail)
R   Red Trail
    (Monadnock Trail)
O   Orange Trail
    (Sunrise Trail)
S   Spur Trail
🚗 Parking

0   .25   .50 Mi

Planning and Precautions

Always carry water and snacks and be aware of the time. Mileage on a map can be deceiving. Walking a mile on level ground takes far less time than hiking a mile on the mountain. Sugarloaf closes at sunset, so plan accordingly. And please, properly dispose of—or better yet, take out—all garbage.

Gnats and mosquitoes can be annoying during the warmer months, so you may need to apply an environmentally friendly repellant to minimize exposure. Also, thoroughly check yourself, your children, and pets for ticks following any outing in the woods. As a precaution, you may want to wear long sleeves and pants even in hot weather. Brush off your clothing before entering your car. Look for all ticks, including the tiniest deer ticks (pinhead size or smaller) that can carry Lyme disease. Remove any attached tick at once with precision (fine-jaw) tweezers by grasping the tick's head as close to the skin as possible. Gently pull out the tick in a straight motion. Be careful not to squeeze the tick's body, which can inject fluid into your skin. Wash the area thoroughly and apply an antiseptic. Your doctor may want you to save the tick for study. Ticks are most active in spring and fall, but they can be encountered at any time. If within four to twenty days following a woodland outing you come down with flu-like symptoms (fever, chills, headache, weakness, fatigue), joint pain, and/or a rash (which may or may not be the classic ring-shaped rash associated with Lyme disease), be sure to consult your doctor immediately, as these could indicate the onset of a tick-borne illness. Early detection is key, and antibiotics are available for treatment.

Two species of venomous snakes—the copperhead and the timber rattler—inhabit Sugarloaf, but are rarely seen. In order to avoid an unsafe encounter, be mindful of where you put your hands and feet (on the trails, on/about rocks, and so forth). In the unlikely event of snakebite, stay calm and seek emergency medical attention. Snake encounters are uncommon on the mountain, and when they do occur, the odds are that the snake is a nonvenomous species such as the black rat snake or ringneck snake. (See p. 77–78 for reptile descriptions.)

Also, the venomous black widow spider occasionally can be seen along the mountain trails. If you encounter one, admire it from a distance.

Black bears are at times seen on or near the mountain, but should present no hazard unless you startle a mother and cubs at close range. Coyotes and mountain lions are also being reported in the area, but both are secretive and pose little threat. However, if you see any animal acting strangely or showing no fear of you, stay away. Nocturnal animals such as raccoons and striped skunks that are out and about in daylight may be rabid. (See p. 74–76 for mammal descriptions.)

Poison ivy is very common on the mountain. The well-maintained trails usually keep it at arm's length, but in some places it grows close to the pathway. Learn to recognize the plant's three-leaflet pattern and thick, hairy, tree-climbing vines. If your hands come in contact with it, be careful not to touch your face. Wash exposed areas thoroughly with soap and water as soon as possible.

Sugarloaf's large rocks are irresistible to children, who begin climbing them the instant they are out of the car. In most cases, the rocks are fairly flat-topped and safe to climb, but keep an eye on young mountaineers and be especially careful when the rocks are wet.

Crime can be a problem anywhere, so don't leave valuables in your car or unattended in other areas. Sugarloaf attracts friendly people who want to enjoy nature, but the mountain exists in the real world and one must always be aware.

Finally, keep a close eye on the weather, and don't underestimate the time it will take for your hike. Plan to be off the mountain before dark, when it closes. Consult the weather forecast before hiking and make sure you will be off the mountain before the onset of thunderstorms, which are common on summer afternoons. Remember that weather in Sugarloaf country can be very different from the weather nearby. When it's drizzling in D.C. or Baltimore, it could be icy, snowy, or even sunny at Sugarloaf.

Trail Etiquette and Stronghold Rules

All natural features of Sugarloaf are protected. Picking plants, disturbing wildlife, and removing rocks from the mountain are prohibited. Alcohol, fires, and overnight camping are not allowed. Remember that this is not a public park but private property that is open to the public during daylight hours.

Please show courtesy to others during your visit, and have a wonderful time!

Short Trails to the Summit

The Green Trail (The A. M. Thomas Trail)

Most people who think of climbing Sugarloaf think of the Green Trail. A steep, quarter-mile climb to the summit, the Green Trail includes a stretch over stone steps that were built many years ago by Sugarloaf's first superintendent, Albert M. Thomas, for whom the trail is named. Gordon Strong posted the following verse at the outset of this trail:

> One quarter mile horizontally
> (But it is not quite horizontal)
> 325 feet vertically
> (But it is not quite vertical either)
> Tentanda est via
> (It is a trail worth trying).

The Green Trail provides dramatic views of the quartzite cliffs just below the summit, cliffs that are frequently populated by rock climbers and all their gear.

The Green Trail begins at West View, where there are picnic tables, portable toilets, and a small, covered wooden shelter. (The rectangular stone structure near the West View parking lot was built as part of Gordon Strong's original West View or "Fourth View." Children often refer to it as the castle and dungeon because of its imposing appearance and dark storage area.) Follow the green blazes, bearing toward the left behind the covered wooden shelter and beyond the Blue Trail. You will quickly begin a gradual climb and then a steeper ascent, culminating in the series of stone steps.

Botanical highlights of the trail include several species of oaks and other mature woodland trees, mountain laurel (which blooms in May and early June), blue-stemmed goldenrod (blossoming near the top of the stone steps in late summer and fall), and witch hazel (blooming in late autumn next to the steps). You may hear the loud "tock" or "quawk" of a raven as you approach the summit on the Green Trail. Ravens have nested here for many years.

The trail is steep and you may be out of breath when you reach the summit, but the view is worth the effort. In the May 1933 issue of *American Motorist,* writer James Alexander described a hike up what is now the Green Trail and the view from the summit:

> This inviting trail leads up to the foot of sheer cliffs which form the crest of Sugar Loaf; here giant boulders, by some mighty convulsion of nature have been strewn around like so many jack-straws; yet so long ago was it that the trees and shrubs have gained a good foothold and have spread wide and tenderly protecting branches above the confusion. The trail has now become steps that are sometimes hewn out of the solid rock or again rock and concrete have been molded into a stairway. All during the ascent there are intriguing glimpses of sugar-white clouds against the blue sky.
>
> The top of Sugar Loaf is about 1,300 feet elevation, but it seems much higher, such a splendid bird's-eye view does it afford of all the surrounding country; great barns and comfortable old farmhouses lie at your feet with the thin line of an old rock fence separating the fields. The blue Catoctins impose their bulk against the sky, ending abruptly at Point of Rocks. . . . A little farther to the left the Potomac gleams like pewter and the old Monocacy aqueduct shows up in silhouette.[1]

Happily, but for the power plant and trash incinerator to the southwest, the view from the top of Sugarloaf still resembles the description put forth by the writer so many decades ago. From the summit of the mountain you look west-northwest over woods and farmland to Catoctin and South Mountains and the mountain gap formed by the Potomac at Point of Rocks, Maryland. You can make out the city of Frederick to the northwest and, to the south, the villages of Dickerson, Barnesville, and Beallsville. Off in the southern distance are the Bull Run Mountains of Virginia and the beginnings of that state's Blue Ridge Mountains in the west and southwest.

The curiously wind-sculpted evergreens growing on the summit are table mountain pines, a species limited to high altitudes of the central Appalachians. Black birch, mountain laurel, and chestnut oak also grow on the summit. Pick a rock with a view and stay a while!

The Orange Trail (The Sunrise Trail)

The Orange Trail is a short, steep, quarter-mile trail that connects to the Red Trail just shy of the summit. The trail originates near the picnic tables and behind the portable toilets at East View. It ascends gradually and then gets very steep for a short section. After that, it again ascends more gradually. This is a fun trail for getting a taste of what climbing big mountains is like. There are large rocks and exposed tree roots to step over, and when you get to the top of the steepest section you can turn around for a farmland view (most dramatic when the leaves are down). The trail is steep enough that anyone with knee problems should probably consider climbing *up* the Orange Trail and then *down* a more gradual connecting trail, or the Green Trail, which has stone steps.

The Orange Trail is a great place to see jack-in-the-pulpits and other April wildflowers. Look for them on both sides of the trail just up from East View. In late May, the mountain laurel display along the trail is spectacular, especially at the steepest sections. Midway up the trail is a clump of bracken fern, and near the intersection with the Red Trail is a mini-forest of mayapple leaves in spring. Look for small clumps of wild geranium in April and May at the intersection of the Orange and Red Trails. In October and November, witch hazel blooms along the Orange Trail.

The Red Trail (The Monadnock Trail)

The Red Trail is a quarter-mile trail linking the Blue Trail and the summit. The Orange Trail intersects with it near the top of the mountain, making the Red Trail a good trail to incorporate into circuit hikes. The Red Trail is moderately steep, but not as steep as the Green or Orange Trails. It begins at the Blue Trail near the Bill Lambert Overlook, an open rock shelf with a spectacular view over the wooded northwestern slopes of the mountain toward Frederick. This is a good place to watch black and turkey vultures and the occasional hawk soaring on the currents. It is also a good spot for viewing the first green blush of spring in the tulip-trees, and then the colors of autumn.

A carpet of hay-scented ferns spreads out on either side of the beginning of the Red Trail. The trail soon begins its climb and is rather steep for a short stretch. Woodland trees here include black birch, red maple, tupelo, chestnut oak, and other oak species. Toward the top of the trail is a rich section of forest that harbors many spring and summer wildflowers: mayapple, yellow corydalis, jack-in-the-pulpit, wild geranium, cleavers, and black cohosh, among others. Unfortunately, an invasive non-native plant called garlic mustard has gotten a foothold here, threatening the lower-growing native wildflowers.

From here the trail ascends gradually to the summit with its panoramic views. Just before reaching the summit you may be greeted by the scent of fringe-tree blossoms if you are hiking in May; there is a delightful mini-forest of these uncommon small trees or large shrubs to the right of the trail. If you began your hike at West View, having taken the Blue Trail to the Red Trail, you can return to West View via the Green Trail (a steep quarter-mile hike back to the parking lot, the beginning of it via stone steps) or you may simply retrace your steps. If you began the hike at East View, having come up the Orange Trail to the Red Trail, you can hike down the Green Trail and then walk along the road from West View to East View, or, consulting the map, you can use other trails to create a longer circuit.

Longer Trails That Are Circular

The Blue Trail (Northern Peaks Trail)

The Blue Trail, a five-mile loop, is a scenic, satisfying, half-day hike that takes you out along Sugarloaf's long, northern ridge and through varied terrain. It offers beautiful views, especially with a few side steps. However, it doesn't go over the highest summit of the mountain, so you will need to use the Green and/or Red Trails to include the summit. This is most easily accomplished by parking at West View, hiking the Green Trail to the summit, and then descending on the Red Trail to Blue.

If you begin at West View and stay on the Blue Trail, you will be on a level stretch that affords dramatic views looking up to Sugarloaf's rocky western front. This tumble of rock is called talus. In earliest spring, trailing arbutus blooms along this stretch of trail. (Be sure to get down on your hands and knees to smell it.) Look also for plantain-leaved pussytoes and violets during early spring. The mountain laurel is spectacular all along this trail in late May.

After passing the Bill Lambert Overlook (see the Red Trail description on p. 53) on your left and the beginning of the Red Trail on your right, you'll begin a descent through rich, rock-strewn woods. Spicebush lines either side of the trail, and jack-in-the-pulpits spring up during April and May. The trail soon intersects with the White Trail. Turn left here and be sure to follow the blue blazes as the Blue Trail soon veers to the right, leaving the White Trail.

After a brief level stretch, the trail veers left and climbs steeply to the northern ridge of Sugarloaf. Members of the heath family grow profusely along the top of the ridge, including blueberries and huckleberries, which ripen during early summer. The inedible deerberry, also growing here, produces larger fruit. After reaching the northern ridge, you will hike along the narrow summit for a good distance, with views to the east (most dramatic in nonfoliated months) and occasionally to the west. Wildflowers grow along the northern ridge from early spring through autumn, although natives are being crowded out by the invasive alien called garlic mustard. This is the only place I know on Sugarloaf where early saxifrage grows. Several species of violets, cut-leaved toothwort, yellow corydalis, and other wildflowers bloom in rich pockets of soil during spring. Black cohosh comes out in June. The tulip-trees create a baby-green glow in spring and then turn yellow and gold in autumn. During the spring months you are almost guaranteed to hear the high, thin, "squeaky-wheel" song of the black-and-white warbler along the northern ridge. Follow the blazes and be careful not to veer off the Blue Trail; in 2000 a fire road was created that crosses the trail.

A highlight of earliest spring on the northern ridge is the common shadbush or serviceberry, a small tree in the rose family that produces creamy blossoms against coppery new leaves during late March or early April. With the rest of the northern slopes still wintry, the blooming of shad against gray-pink rock is a scene of subtle beauty.

When you reach the stretch of trail with very large rocks to the left, be sure to climb them. The rocks themselves are beautifully contoured, and you will look down over the western wooded slopes. Here I have seen small lizards called five-lined skinks (and possibly even the larger broad-headed skink, although it made too quick a getaway for positive identification). Blueberries and huckleberries grow along here, and the wind-gnarled table mountain pine.

The trail then descends through a thick grove of mountain laurel. You will cross the Yellow Trail and begin the ascent toward White Rocks. A rocky, winding trail through pine and laurel, blueberry and huckleberry, this is one of the wildest, least crowded sections of trail on Sugarloaf. With the leaves down, you will catch glimpses back to the summit of the mountain. The views here are so pristinely wooded that it's easy to imagine yourself in a more remote part of the Appalachians. The trail ascends gradually, then more steeply, and soon tops a height of land. Here is a pile of stones called a cairn. It is traditional for a hiker to add one stone per hike to the rock pile.

The trail then descends a bit, winding around toward White Rocks. Look for wildflowers; during late April or early May you may see pink lady's slippers blooming. If you do, remember to leave the plants undisturbed. Just before the final ascent toward White Rocks is a rich section of woods that gives rise to many spring wildflowers, including cut-leaved toothwort and jack-in-the-pulpit.

A short spur leads out to White Rocks, which affords a spectacular view to the west and northwest. Be sure to explore not only the rocks just in front of you, but also the rocky outcrop that is a short walk to the right (as you are facing west). You will be looking down to Lilypons Water Gardens and Adamstown, Buckeystown, and the city of Frederick beyond. Catoctin and South Mountains are the long blue ridges on the horizon.

When you leave White Rocks, be sure you are continuing on the Blue Trail loop and not backtracking. (This trail's intersection can be confusing. Do not follow the sign pointing to the left that says "West View Parking" unless you want to retrace your steps. Heading toward Mount Ephraim Road continues the loop that will bring you back to West View.) The trail descends, is level, ascends and winds around to the left, and then descends, bearing toward the right and, with another small up and down, to Mount Ephraim Road. Follow the blue blazes along the road to the left, where you will wade through one of the small, shallow tributaries of Bear Branch. The road makes a right turn (this is a Yellow Trail crossing), passing over a second Bear Branch tributary. A small wetland to your left, just before Bear Branch, is worth checking out. During spring it sports dog violets and many other wildflowers; during summer, agrimony; and in autumn, great blue lobelia. To the right, on the other side of the road, you will find maple-leaved viburnum. Cinnamon fern, sensitive fern, and royal fern all grow in this charming little wetland. If you have time, a walk along Mount Ephraim Road in either direction will probably yield wildflower sightings from spring through fall.

As the Blue Trail turns left off Mount Ephraim Road, it runs adjacent to a beautiful stretch of the Bear Branch tributary you have just crossed. Cinnamon ferns form a lush backdrop for Indian cucumber root and other spring wildflowers, including an orchid called large whorled pogonia. These uncommon plants must be fiercely protected. The trail gradually ascends through mature beeches and other woodland trees. To the left you will see a myriad of tropical-looking skunk cabbage leaves during the spring as you hear the trickle of the creek. Spicebush grows along the creek, forming a haze of yellow blossoms in early spring and spicy red berrylike drupes in autumn. This is a good place to hear resident birds such as the ovenbird, wood thrush, red-eyed vireo, eastern towhee, scarlet tanager, and Louisiana waterthrush. You are also apt to hear the dry trill of a worm-eating warbler. During the spring migration this stretch of the Blue Trail and Mount Ephraim Road are teeming with migrants.

The trail winds to the right, leaving the creek and its springs, and climbs a little more steeply to a rocky stretch lined with mountain laurel. Several wildflower species pop up here and there during spring and summer. The trail then joins the White Trail again. Turn right and follow the blue and white blazes along a fairly level but rocky stretch. The trail turns left and climbs steeply (look for trailing arbutus on the right); at the top of this ascent look for the Blue Trail to veer left and away from the White Trail. A very steep but blessedly short climb will take you back to West View and your car. During late April and early May you may find some pink lady's slippers at trail's end.

The White Trail (The Mountain Loop Trail)

The White Trail is a two-and-a-half-mile circuit that begins near the parking lot at the mountain base. From the White Trail you may connect with any other Sugarloaf Mountain trail, directly or indirectly. The White Trail affords a beautiful mountain hike with a lot of climbing, some of it steep. The entire hike is spent in scenic woodlands. To see views you will have to veer off the trail.

Begin by passing through the mountain gate, then follow the mountain road as it passes between two wooden buildings (once a contiguous horse and carriage barn). Here you may see chimney swifts (some birders call them "cigars on wings") and barn swallows swooping overhead. The "chur" of a red-bellied woodpecker may be heard. You can pick up a map from a holder on the wall of the building to your left. You will walk under several tall white pines as you begin a gradual ascent. As you pass under the pine boughs, begin looking for white blazes on the trees in front of you that, for a short while, coincide with yellow blazes. Wildflowers grow along the roadside from spring to fall. Look for a dirt and gravel road on your left. The White Trail veers immediately off from the right side of this road and is well marked with a double white blaze.

You will find yourself in a forest with many mature trees, among them oaks, hickories, American beech, red maple, tupelo, tulip-tree, and a few sassafras (and, perhaps, flowering dogwood that has survived the blight). September's first color—a peach, orange, and scarlet blush in the tupelo trees—and November's last hurrah—the flaming up of the red and scarlet oaks—can be seen in these woods, with other oaks, hickories, red maple, dogwood, sassafras, and tulip-trees adding their own hues.

The White Trail is flanked by many members of the heath family that thrive in Sugarloaf's acidic soils. The trail is lined with evergreen mountain laurel, blooming in May and early June, and a few specimens of the earlier, deciduous pink azalea or pinxter flower. Edible blueberries and huckleberries and the closely related (but inedible) deerberry grow along semi-open stretches of the White Trail, and hugging the earth are the leathery evergreen leaves and sweet-smelling early spring blossoms of the trailing arbutus.

As the trail begins its climb, look for pink lady's slippers in late April and early May and, close to the forest floor, the whorled evergreen leaves of the striped or spotted wintergreen plant, which blooms in June. Also listen for the high dry trill of the worm-eating warblers nesting here during spring and early summer. You are apt to hear the loud call of the pileated woodpecker from the White Trail, and it is a good trail for songbirds during spring and summer, including ovenbirds, red-eyed vireos, eastern wood-pewees, scarlet tanagers, eastern towhees, and—especially once you reach the western side of the mountain—rose-breasted grosbeaks. As you continue your ascent, a large rocky outcrop is visible through the trees slightly to your left. You will come upon some scrub (or Virginia) pines, and then the trail crosses the road.

For many years a single specimen of wild indigo has grown close to the trail to your left. It produces yellow flowers during early summer. Slightly farther along the trail you'll find other late spring- and summer-flowering plants, including the lovely pink pasture or Carolina rose. After a fairly level stretch with gradual ups and downs, the trail begins its steepest pitch through large patches of huckleberry and blueberry, edible in summer, their leaves a scarlet carpet in autumn. At the top of this steep climb, you'll veer sharply right to continue on the White Trail. A white diamond trail to the left is a short walk to East View, where you'll find picnic tables, portable toilets, and pleasing views of Comus, Barnesville, and the surrounding farmland.

The tree community changes a little here, with black birch and tulip-tree more prominent. You'll notice this especially in autumn, when the early gold of the birches and then the butter yellow of the tulip-trees contribute to Sugarloaf's fall palette. Watch your step all along the White Trail in autumn, when it is peppered with acorns.

After a descent and a long, gradual ascent, the trail levels, and then you intersect briefly with the Blue Trail. Pay careful attention to the blazes along this stretch. During mid to late spring look for wild sarsaparilla and, as the White Trail turns left away from the Blue Trail, jack-in-the-pulpit. You'll climb to a level area that is carpeted with pale green hay-scented fern, whose fronds turn yellow and bronze during early autumn. Begin descending and look for more jack-in-the-pulpit and, in early spring, the delicately stalked rue anemone. A few rattlesnake ferns also grow here. In late September and October you will find yourself among a blaze of tupelo leaves. Be careful to stay on the trail, as fire roads intersect it here.

This stretch is level for some time. The Blue Trail again intersects with the White Trail for a fairly long distance, so keep track of the white blazes. This is a gorgeous stretch when the mountain laurel is blooming. The trail will veer left and climb rather steeply to where the Blue Trail departs the White Trail (heading up to West View, where there are picnic tables, portable toilets, and views to the west). Stay on the White Trail and you will descend. Wildflowers bloom here from spring through fall, including dittany, bearing lavender flowers during late summer and early fall. A white diamond trail to the left will take you to Potomac Overlook, with views to the southwest. If you stay on the White Trail you will continue to descend to a clearing with an old cabin to your right. During mid to late spring violet wood sorrel grows along this stretch of trail. Look for a spring-fed creek to your left, a good spot for cinnamon and royal ferns and wetland wildflowers.

After continuing to descend and paralleling the creek for a short distance, you cross the creek and the trail levels out. Soon after, you join the Yellow Trail as it comes in from the right and becomes one with the White Trail. Continue straight on the combined trails until they reach the road down the mountain near its intersection with Comus Road. To stay on the White Trail turn left on the road, ascend for a short distance, and look for a White and Yellow Trail turn-off on your right. From here it is a short walk along a partially paved trail back to the road up the mountain, where you will complete the White Trail loop, then turn right to follow the road between the two wooden buildings and back to your vehicle.

A short side trip from the last stretch of the White Trail takes you to the Strong Memorial Garden, a formal garden recently revitalized to honor the memory of Gordon Strong and two Stronghold board members. From the paved path connecting the two mountain roads, look for a tree-lined lane climbing up to your left just before you reach the stone foundation with three picnic tables. Follow this inviting lane a short way, and you will be in a stone-walled garden surrounded by weeping spruce trees. The garden was renovated by Stronghold during and after the year 2000 in a spot where a pool and formal garden had been. From here you can see sweeping views of the Strong Mansion and Westwood, another stately home just south of it. In the garden you get a feeling for the opulence and grace of Gordon Strong's former home and landscaped surroundings. As you return to the White Trail, straight ahead you will see the hill where Gordon and Louise Strong are buried in a stone mausoleum. The mausoleum is beyond an old stone fireplace and chimney. It formerly was surrounded by tall trees, but a windstorm with tornadic force took down many of the trees in 1977. Stronghold has created a rock and flower garden near the Strongs' resting place.

The Yellow Trail (The Saddleback Horse Trail)

The Yellow Trail is Sugarloaf's longest trail, a seven-mile loop that is open to horseback riders and (on weekdays from May through November only) mountain bikers. The trail meanders through wetlands, crossing creeks and passing several springs, and because of this it affords glimpses of many wetland plants. Wildflowers bloom along the Yellow Trail from spring through fall. You will find cinnamon, sensitive, and royal ferns in the wettest spots and New York ferns in areas that are merely moist. Other fern species may be seen along the way, among them rattlesnake ferns, hay-scented ferns, intermediate wood ferns, lady ferns, and, especially on the western side of the mountain, Christmas ferns.

There are several places to access the Yellow Trail, but parking is limited everywhere. If you begin at the mountain base (where you are most likely to find parking), walk through the mountain gate and follow the paved road for a short way. You will pass between two wooden buildings and under some tall white pines. Begin looking for yellow blazes on the trees. Shortly after the White Trail veers off to the left, the road begins to climb and is flanked by a low stone wall on the right. After a short walk the Yellow Trail veers off the road to your right. There is a wooden marker at the spot that says "Saddleback Horse Trail." (This is a new trail access as of 2001.) The trail heads downhill through a forest of young tulip-trees. Other trees found along this first stretch of trail include pines, hickories, red maples, and chestnut, red, and white oaks.

The trail meanders through wooded and cleared stretches, with changing plant communities. The Yellow Trail has been widened for selective logging in various places, and soil disruption has opened the way for invasive species. The bright green grass you see along many open sections is called Japanese stilt grass *(Microstegium vimineum)*. Pretty to look at, it is an invasive grass that crowds out native plants. You also will see perilla, an Asian mint family member that has become a threat to native plant communities, and the ubiquitous, invasive garlic mustard.

In cleared stretches of the Yellow Trail look for summer and fall wildflowers such as common mullein and members of the aster or daisy family (black-eyed Susan, ox-eye daisy, fall asters and goldenrods, and New York ironweed). Blackberries, dewberries, and wineberries grow along cleared sections of the trail. You may also see the diminutive, four-petaled blossom of the sprawling summer-blooming plant called St. Andrew's cross. Spring-blooming violets also are common along the Yellow Trail, in both open and wooded stretches, and rue anemone grows in some wooded sections.

Because it connects with active logging sites, the Yellow Trail varies from a woodland path to a wider, sometimes graveled road. After about a thirty-minute walk, the trail passes a spring on the left. Just above the spring is an old black birch with sprawling gnarled roots wrapped around rocks and reaching toward the spring. Look for cinnamon ferns and jack-in-the-pulpits during spring. (These jack-in-the-pulpits are a later-blooming variety that once was considered a separate species.) On both sides of the trail at this intersection the intriguing seedbox, with its yellow summer flowers and small, box-like fruit, can be found, if it hasn't been disturbed by trail widening. You may also see a monkey flower in bloom during the summer, or turtlehead (host plant for the Baltimore checkerspot butterfly) during fall. Jewelweed grows in the spring, and along the trail here and there are large clusters of Chinese bushclover that bloom during summer and fall.

The trail (which is wide here) crosses one or more creeks, depending on seasonal rains, and then begins to veer left and ascend, at first gradually and then steeply. The trail makes several turns, and because of the numerous logging roads that crisscross the area, you will want to make sure you are following the yellow blazes. Near the

Black birch tree above a Sugarloaf spring

trail's highest point is a rich section of woods harboring many spring wildflowers, including violets and two species of toothwort. The trail circles around to an intersection with the Blue Trail. (A left turn here on Blue will lead you to the highest elevations of Sugarloaf's long northern ridge, and a right turn on Blue will take you to White Rocks.) Continuing on Yellow, you follow a fire road, which gradually descends. During spring you may see pinxter flower (or wild pink azalea) in bloom and, a little later, mountain laurel. Pink lady's slippers and Christmas and New York ferns grow along the fire road. The trail crosses a tributary of Bear Branch and then runs alongside this small creek to Mount Ephraim Road. Here are beautiful American beech trees.

Follow the yellow blazes along Mount Ephraim Road until the Yellow Trail goes off into the woods to your right. This next section of trail passes through Stronghold's forestry demonstration area, where you can observe the impacts of various forestry methods (see p. 45 for a description). The plants you see will vary according to whether the habitat has been logged. After a while you will begin to veer left, and then you will cross a tributary of Furnace Branch. Look here for Canada mayflower (or wild lily of the valley) during spring. This is also a good place to see cinnamon and royal fern. After a brief time you come to Mount Ephraim Road again. A cleared opening just before the road is home to many late-spring- and summer-blooming flowers. Coltsfoot, with its small, dandelionlike flower heads, blooms here in late winter and earliest spring. Later, after the flower is gone, you may see its colt's-foot-shaped basal leaves. Cross Mount Ephraim Road and, again, pay careful attention to the blazes.

The trail meanders through woodland and reaches a confusing intersection where yellow blazes go off to left and right. A right turn will take you back to Mount Ephraim Road; a left turn will continue the Yellow Trail loop. Turn left, descend toward a creek crossing, and then go right at the intersection with the White Trail. The Yellow and White Trails coincide along a level stretch and bring you to the road down the mountain just before it ends at Comus Road. Go left on the mountain road and climb a few yards until you see the Yellow and White Trails veering to the right on a partially paved trail. Follow this trail back to the road up the mountain, where you will turn right, pass between the double wooden buildings, and return to your vehicle.

The Yellow Trail also can be accessed from limited parking areas on Sugarloaf Mountain Road and Mount Ephraim Road. Please be careful not to block entrances to fire roads or interfere with traffic on these small rustic roads.

Hiking the Monocacy Natural Resources Management Area

The Monocacy Natural Resources Management Area comprises twenty-one hundred acres of forest and farm fields immediately adjacent to Stronghold property and stretching from Maryland Route 28 to Ed Sears Road. Furnace Branch (former site of the Johnson brothers' iron furnace) flows into the Monocacy River within the Monocacy Natural Resources Management Area, which is administered by the Maryland Department of Natural Resources. Lying within this area, just west of Sugarloaf, is a long, narrow, wooded ridge with a few rocky places..

Mature forests harboring many species of wildflowers are crisscrossed by unblazed bridle trails often used by local equestrians and hunters. It's easy to get lost in these woods, and hunting is legal here with a permit. But the woodlands lining Furnace Branch are a desirable destination for anyone who loves wildflowers. Dwarf ginseng, trout lily, spring beauty, and many other spring ephemerals line the rich banks of the creek. During spring migration, this is an excellent birding spot. There is a dramatic stand of old hemlocks in a scenic, rocky stretch of Furnace Branch; unfortunately, the trees are dying, victims of the latest tree plague, a small Asian insect pest called the woolly adelgid.

Parts of the Monocacy Natural Resources Management Area are still farmed, and history buffs may be able to locate the remains of the old quarries, a lime kiln, and other reminders of Sugarloaf's industrial past. This area, off the beaten path, is an interesting mix of habitats, and stretches of Furnace Branch are breathtakingly beautiful. The area can be accessed from Mount Ephraim Road, Route 28 near the Monocacy Bridge, and Ed Sears Road. If you venture into this area, pay close attention to landmarks so you will be able to trace your steps.

Spring-blooming plants (mountain laurel, pinxter flower, trailing arbutus, bloodroot, star chickweed, jack-in-the-pulpit, Canada mayflower, perfoliate bellwort, Solomon's seal, marsh blue violet, spring beauty, rattlesnake weed, round-lobed hepatica, sweet cicely)

4 Plants of Sugarloaf Mountain

Sugarloaf Mountain is home to several hundred woody and herbaceous plant species, all of which are described in detail and shown in our forthcoming companion volume, *An Illustrated Guide to Eastern Woodland Wildflowers and Trees: 350 Plants Observed at Sugarloaf Mountain, Maryland.* In addition, many plants are mentioned in chapter 3, "Sugarloaf's Trail System," and chapter 6, "Sugarloaf Country through the Seasons."

The observant visitor will find plants blooming nearly year-round on the mountain, from the first skunk cabbage of late winter to the last witch hazel flowers of autumn. The Sugarloaf area encompasses a number of different habitats and soil types, supporting a broad range of species. Plants indigenous to the Mid-Atlantic Coastal Plain, Piedmont, and mountain regions overlap here. Because of the pristine nature of Sugarloaf's woodlands, rare and threatened species find valuable habitat, including two orchids that are considered threatened species in Maryland: the yellow-fringed orchid *(Platanthera ciliaris)* and the large purple-fringed orchid *(Platanthera grandiflora).*

Members of the heath family thrive in Sugarloaf's acidic soils. Mountain laurel *(Kalmia latifolia)* is a May–June blooming evergreen shrub that is ubiquitous on the mountain's slopes. Its pink and white snowball-shaped blossom clusters blanket the mountain in peak blooming years. Memorial Day, or the week or two leading up to it, usually is a reliable time for Sugarloaf's mountain laurel display. Other heath family members that thrive here include the fragrant, diminutive trailing arbutus (Epigaea repens), which is among the mountain's earliest spring wildflowers; the pinxter flower (or wild pink azalea) (Rhododendron periclymenoides); and the uncommon wintergreen (Gaultheria procumbens).

The incomparably beautiful pink lady's slipper (Cypripedium acaule), an orchid family member, also favors Sugarloaf's acidic soils. In addition to the two threatened species already mentioned, several other orchids bloom in Sugarloaf's woods in a number of different habitats from spring through fall.

Early spring wildflowers favoring the richer, more basic soils of Sugarloaf's streamsides and some trail sections include bloodroot (Sanguinaria canadensis), cut-leaved toothwort (Cardamine concatenata) and slender toothwort (Cardamine angustata), rue anemone (Anemonella thalictroides), and round-lobed hepatica (Hepatica americana). A little later in the spring, rich soils support smooth Solomon's seal (Polygonatum biflorum) and false Solomon's seal (Smilacina racemosa), Canada mayflower (Maianthemum canadense), and Indian cucumber root (Medeola virginiana). A variety of spring violets (Viola) have adapted to almost every habitat, some favoring wet and some favoring dry situations. Violet wood sorrel (Oxalis violacea), jack-in-the-pulpit (Arisaema triphyllum), wild sarsaparilla (Aralia nudicaulis), and partridgeberry (Mitchella repens) also bloom alongside some trails.

During the summer and early fall, many members of the mint family, including skullcaps (Scutellaria spp.), wild basil (Satureja vulgaris), and dittany (Cunila origanoides), bloom on Sugarloaf. Late summer and fall are dominated by aster or daisy family members, such as goldenrod (Solidago spp.), asters (Aster), and Eupatoriums (Eupatorium). Several Lobelia species also bloom during summer and fall, including the brilliant red cardinal flower (L. cardinalis).

Oaks and hickories dominate the mountain forests. The chestnut oak (Quercus prinus) is probably the most predominant tree on the mountain. Other Sugarloaf trees include tulip-tree (Liriodendron tulipifera), American beech (Fagus grandifolia), red maple (Acer rubrum), tupelo (Nyssa sylvatica), common shadbush (Amelanchier arborea), flowering dogwood (Cornus florida), redbud (Cercis canadensis), and black locust (Robinia pseudoacacia). Black birch (Betula lenta) grows at the highest elevations. Sugarloaf's most dramatic tree is the table mountain pine *(Pinus pungens)*. This smallish tree grows mostly in the mountains, and in a limited range from New Jersey and Pennsylvania to northern Georgia. The trees favor rocky, wind-swept outcrops, and they become stunted and sculpted by the wind to resemble the shapes of bonsai trees. The picturesque appearance of Sugarloaf's summit is due largely to table mountain pines and the way they complement the mountain's pink quartzite.

Numerous shrubs and vines also call these slopes home. Shrubs include two with wispy yellow flowers: the early-spring-blooming spicebush *(Lindera benzoin)* of Sugarloaf's streamsides, and the late-autumn-flowering common witch hazel *(Hamamelis virginiana)*, a small tree or shrub that grows beside most trails. The spring-flowering fringe-tree *(Chionanthus virginicus)* is a large shrub or small tree bearing fragrant, airy blossom clusters. Vines include wild grapes *(Vitis)*, poison ivy *(Rhus radicans)*, Virginia creeper *(Parthenocissus quinquefolia)*, trumpet creeper *(Campsis radicans)*, common greenbrier *(Smilax rotundifolia)*, and Japanese honeysuckle *(Lonicera japonica)*, a ubiquitous invasive.

Pink lady's slipper

5 Sugarloaf Wildlife

Birds

Sugarloaf and its surroundings have long been a mecca for birders in the Mid-Atlantic region. In her local classic *Finding Birds in the National Capital Area* (revised edition, 1992), Claudia Wilds wrote: "There is hardly a better area [in the capital region] to bird west of the Chesapeake Bay than southern Frederick County in Maryland. . . . On a fine day in May it is not hard to find one hundred species in the course of twelve hours or so, if you reach the foot of Sugarloaf Mountain early enough to hear the Great Horned Owls, Eastern Screech-Owls, and Whip-poor-wills."[1]

Avian spring in Sugarloaf country begins as early as Valentine's Day with the lusty song of the northern cardinal *(Cardinalis cardinalis)*. Soon after, the red-winged blackbirds *(Agelaius phoeniceus)* begin calling out "conkaree" from farmland fields and ponds ringing the mountain. Around the first of March the song sparrow *(Melospiza melodia)* begins singing, and then the eastern phoebe *(Sayornis phoebe)* returns to nest in the eaves of the buildings at the mountain base. March is the month of the strange and wonderful spiral flight of the American woodcock *(Scolopax minor)*, a mating ritual occurring in farm fields and wet meadows across the region.

The succession of migrating and returning birds is almost as reliable as the succession of spring wildflowers. The spring migration peaks in late April and May as waves of warblers grace Sugarloaf country with their brilliant feathers and pleasing songs. On a May morning more than a dozen warbler species may be found on and near the mountain. Although most are spring migrants, several warbler species remain to breed on and around the mountain, including the ovenbird *(Seiurus aurocapillus)*, the black-and-white warbler *(Mniotilta varia)*, the worm-eating warbler *(Helmitheros vermivora)*, the Louisiana waterthrush *(Seiurus motacilla)*, and the uncommon yellow-breasted chat *(Icteria virens)*.

It's easy to learn some of the common songs you will hear during spring and early-summer visits to the mountain. The eastern towhee *(Pipilo erythrophthalmus)* sings, quite clearly, "drink your tea." The little ovenbird sings a great big "teacher, teacher, teacher"; the eastern phoebe intones a rather harsh "fee-bee"; and the eastern wood-pewee *(Contopus virens)* sings an extremely sweet "pee-a-wee." With a little imagination you can hear the words "see me, here I am" in the song of the red-eyed vireo *(Vireo olivaceus)*. Two nesting warblers have distinctive songs: the worm-eating warbler lets out a high, dry trill, sounding like a loud insect, and the black-and-white warbler's high, thin song has been likened to a squeaky wheel. If you

Wood thrush

drive down Mount Ephraim Road you are almost certain to hear a crisp, distinctive "pizza!" or "pizze!" The "pizza bird," as it is sometimes affectionately called, is the Acadian flycatcher *(Empidonax virescens)*.

If you are familiar with the song of the American robin *(Turdus migratorius)*, it is a small leap to add two additional songs to your birder's repertoire. The rose-breasted grosbeak *(Pheucticus ludovicianus)* sounds like a sweeter robin, and the scarlet tanager *(Piranga olivacea)* sounds like a robin with a sore throat. That loud jungle call off in the distance is probably a yellow-billed cuckoo *(Coccyzus americanus)*, and the mystical, flutelike music in the trees above is the song of the wood thrush *(Hylocichla mustelina)*.

If you linger on the mountain late in the day during spring and summer you may hear the song of the whip-poor-will *(Caprimulgus vociferus)*—sounding just like the name. Once a hallmark of spring and summer nights, the whip-poor-will song is now a rarity, but visitors can still hear these birds on and around Sugarloaf.

Common raven

Several large birds are year-round residents of Sugarloaf. At the mountain summit you will undoubtedly notice large birds soaring on the wind currents. These are two species of vulture—turkey vulture *(Cathartes aura)* and black vulture *(Coragyps atratus)*—who defy their reputation as lowly scavengers with their winged grace. You may hear a loud "tock" or "quawk" as you stand on the summit. Look around for a bird resembling a crow. This is the common raven *(Corvus corax)*, which nests on Sugarloaf and probably nowhere else nearby. Wild turkeys *(Meleagris gallopavo)* are occasionally spotted along the mountain's roads and trails, and the large pileated woodpecker *(Dryocopus pileatus)* is one of several woodpecker species often sighted on the mountain. Canada geese *(Branta canadensis)* have become year-round residents, and goslings are born every year at the pond at the mountain base.

Sugarloaf is home to the large great horned owl *(Bubo virginianus)* and the small eastern screech-owl *(Otus asio)*, which is occasionally seen in the branches overhanging Mount Ephraim Road. Barred owls *(Strix varia)* live in the bottomlands nearby, and the uncommon short-eared owl *(Asio flammeus)* winters in a site just to the west of the mountain.

Great blue herons *(Ardea herodias)* and green herons *(Butorides virescens)* are frequent visitors to Sugarloaf farm ponds. Don't be surprised if a great blue heron comes crashing down through the trees to land on the banks of a heavily wooded Bear Branch. Along this same stretch of Bear Branch you might see a Louisiana or northern waterthrush *(Seiurus noveboracensis)* dancing up and down the creek bank.

Sugarloaf is a good spot from which to observe the fall hawk migration. Red-tailed hawks *(Buteo jamaicensis)*, American kestrels *(Falco sparverius)*, and Cooper's hawks *(Accipiter cooperii)* are frequently seen all year.

Sugarloaf's winter flock includes the Carolina chickadee *(Poecile carolinensis)*, white-breasted nuthatch *(Sitta carolinensis)*, tufted titmouse *(Baeolophus bicolor)*, and downy woodpecker *(Picoides pubescens)*. (All are year-round residents.) Winter is probably the best time to hear and observe the loud and brightly colored pileated woodpecker. If you're lucky you might see and hear a V of tundra swans

(Cygnus columbianus) flying overhead on their way to or from Lilypons, a large water garden. Sugarloaf commands the epicenter of some famous birding spots. On the western side of the mountain the pools at Lilypons are a favorite spot for birders, as are nearby New Design and Oland Roads. Horned larks *(Eremophila alpestris)*, Lapland longspurs *(Calcarius lapponicus)*, and snow buntings *(Plectrophenax nivalis)* congregate in the farm fields near these roads south of Buckeystown. Rare birds are occasionally spotted here; in recent years a gyrfalcon *(Falco rusticolus)* and a snowy owl *(Nyctea scandiaca)* have caused traffic jams. Migrant bobolinks *(Dolichonyx oryzivorus)* can be observed here during spring. South of Sugarloaf there is good year-round birding along the Potomac River and the C&O Canal towpath, and to the southeast the reservoir at Black Hill Regional Park is a great place to observe winter waterfowl and, with luck, bald eagles *(Haliaeetus leucocephalus)*.

Mammals

The white-tailed deer *(Odocoileus virginianus)* resides on and around Sugarloaf Mountain in large numbers. While seeing white-tailed deer was a special occurrence just a few decades ago, these hoofed animals are now so common that they are having a severely negative impact on native plants, farm crops, and area roads (where frequent collisions occur). White-tailed deer browse on the leaves, twigs, and fruits of trees, shrubs, and herbaceous plants. Mating occurs in autumn, and females bear young in the spring. It is common to see deer in herds of several to several dozen on and around the mountain.

Other commonly seen mammals include the gray squirrel *(Sciurus carolinensis)*, which reaps the bounty of Sugarloaf's oaks and other trees (both for food and nesting sites), and the eastern chipmunk *(Tamias striatus)*, a ground dweller. The southern flying squirrel *(Glaucomys volans)*, an impressive glider, resides here but is nocturnal.

Most area mammals are primarily nocturnal and therefore rarely seen by Sugarloaf visitors. These include the Virginia or common opossum, striped skunk, and raccoon, which are all most apt to be seen during nighttime drives along roads encircling the mountain. The Virginia opossum *(Didelphis virginiana)* is the only marsupial in the United States. It nests in burrows, hollow logs, and trees and thrives on a variety of foods, including small mammals, carrion, eggs, fruits, and insects. The striped skunk *(Mephitis mephitis)* hunts at night, dining on rodents, insects, and fruits. The raccoon *(Procyon lotor)*, also primarily nocturnal, eats fish and crayfish (both plentiful in Bear Branch), as well as birds, eggs, fruits, and other plant materials. If you spot these animals during daylight hours, keep a safe distance, as rabies causes nocturnal animals to change their habits.

Both red and gray foxes reside on and around Sugarloaf. The red fox *(Vulpes vulpes)* has become prevalent in Sugarloaf farm country and is often seen in the late afternoon hunting for the small mammals that make up part of its diet (along with snakes, insects, and fruits). The gray fox *(Urocyon cinereoargenteus)* shares a similar diet and also is common around Sugarloaf. It is more exclusively nocturnal than the red fox, so is seen less often. The coyote *(Canis latrans)*, another North American carnivore and fellow member of the dog family *(Canidae)*, has made recent inroads into Maryland, including Frederick and Montgomery Counties. Coyotes have been spotted on and around Sugarloaf.

Other common mammals of Sugarloaf farm country include the ubiquitous eastern cottontail *(Sylvilagus floridanus)*, most active early and late in the day, and the woodchuck or groundhog *(Marmota monax)*. Several species of bats take to area skies at night.

Beavers *(Castor canadensis)* are common here, their whereabouts easily detected by gnawed, fallen trees and their quickly but expertly

Chipmunk

Eastern cottontail

constructed dams. Signs of beaver are found along Furnace Branch in the Monocacy Natural Resources Management Area. This animal, the largest rodent in the United States, has been an invaluable part of the ecosystem across the continent, with its ability to create widespread wetlands from small streams. Its penchant for changing the landscape, however, has also made it an unwelcome resident in many places. The beaver is active early and late in the day, its broad tail sounding the alarm with a resounding slap on the water when danger approaches. In addition to beavers, woodchucks, squirrels, and chipmunks, many smaller rodents such as mice and voles inhabit area woodlands and farms.

Black bears *(Ursus americanus)* increasingly have been spotted on both sides of the mountain in recent years. It's remotely possible you may see the secretive bobcat *(Lynx rufus)* and the mountain lion *(Felis concolor)*. The latter appears to be making a comeback in the area; a mountain lion was sighted on two Barnesville farm properties during the early spring of 2002.

Reptiles

Snakes

Although they are rarely seen, Maryland's only two venomous snake species inhabit Sugarloaf Mountain: the timber rattlesnake *(Crotalus horridus)* and the copperhead *(Agkistrodon contortrix)*. Both snakes are pit vipers, with a sensory facial pit on either side of the head. They are horizontally banded: the timber rattler dark (sometimes almost black) or yellowish green, with a prominent rattle, and the copper-

Black rat snake

head alternating shades of darker and lighter copper. Young copperheads have yellow-tipped tails. If you are lucky enough to see either one, keep a respectful distance and admire it from afar. Sugarloaf's rocky wooded slopes provide invaluable habitat for these snakes, with an abundance of small mammals, birds, and amphibians for food. Copperheads also eat insects. Development has spelled extirpation for the once common timber rattlesnake throughout much of its range in the northeastern United States, and so Sugarloaf has become an important refuge.

A Sugarloaf hiker is more likely to see one of three nonvenomous snakes. The black rat snake *(Elaphe obsoleta obsoleta)*—a long, slender snake that is a uniform black above (or with barely visible paler markings) and white below the throat—is common on and around the mountain. A constrictor whose food sources include mice and birds, the black rat snake is an excellent tree climber. The much smaller ringneck snake *(Diadophis punctatus)* has a thin golden ring below the head. The ringneck snake is a dark bluish-gray above and yellow below. This small, slender species thrives on salamanders, earthworms, lizards, and frogs. Although several other snakes are indigenous to the area, the only one regularly seen by Sugarloaf visitors is the common garter snake *(Thamnophis sirtalis)*.

Turtles

The eastern box turtle *(Terrapene carolina)*—with its high, rounded shell and decorative orange or yellow markings—often is spotted on or along Sugarloaf's hiking trails. This is the only native turtle regularly found far from water. Its foods include worms, insects, snails, and fruits. You may also see a common snapping turtle *(Chelydra serpentina)* on or near the seeps and creeks of Mount Ephraim Road. With its large head and dark rough shell, the omnivorous snapping turtle is easily identified. Keep a safe distance should you see a snapping turtle. If alarmed, it can deliver a fierce bite.

Lizards

A Sugarloaf hiker may encounter a small lizard called a five-lined skink *(Eumeces fasciatus)*. The young are born black or nearly black with five prominent white or yellowish vertical stripes and a bright blue tail. Adults lose the blue tail color, and females lighten in color but usually retain some striping. Males often lose their stripes and become brown with coppery red heads. Another species, the broad-headed skink *(E. laticeps)*, closely resembles the male five-lined skink and may be found on the mountain. Skink food includes insects, spiders, earthworms, and snails.

Amphibians

Frogs and Toads

Several frog species inhabit Sugarloaf area wetlands. The most musical among them are the tiny tree frogs called spring peepers *(Pseudacris crucifer)*. These diminutive gray-green or reddish-brown frogs have a darker X marking on their backs. From their perches near

Spring peeper

area ponds, streams, and swamps, spring peepers begin their collective mating calling during earliest spring. On the first warm evening in March (or even late February), the spring peeper chorus rises from all the wetlands ringing Sugarloaf. The collective song of the spring peeper has been likened to the ringing of sleigh bells. It is a joyous sound, one that accompanies bursting red maple buds, the "conkaree" of the red-winged blackbird, and other familiar signs of spring. Spring peepers sing well into the night for several weeks.

Even earlier than the spring peepers, another local frog chorus can be heard. Wood frogs *(Rana sylvatica),* smallish frogs with dark eye masks, have a short, frenetic late-winter mating period during which they can be heard collectively clucking or quacking in area ponds and pools.

Slightly warmer spring nights also bring forth the surprisingly musical serenade of the lowly American toad *(Bufo americanus).* Beginning in early spring soon after the peepers begin vocalizing, toads sound a high trill lasting up to thirty seconds and collectively sweet sounding. Toads frequently are found along Sugarloaf's hiking trails, to the delight of children.

Later spring and summer evenings in Sugarloaf country are punctuated by the sounds of calling frogs, including the rumbling "garumph" of the large bullfrog *(Rana catesbeiana)* and the distinctive twang (like a banjo) of the green frog *(Rana clamitans).* The pickerel frog *(Rana palustris)* has a spring call that has been likened to a snore. The common gray treefrog *(Hyla versicolor)* has a call that sounds like that of a red-bellied woodpecker. The common gray treefrog's warbling "chur" is heard well into summer in Sugarloaf country.

Salamanders

Ponds and vernal pools in Sugarloaf country attract large numbers of spotted salamanders *(Ambystoma maculatum)* during early spring. Spotted salamanders, which are black with yellow spots, spend much of their lives underground. As soon as the weather warms they travel to area waters, where they congregate for a communal mating ritual involving considerable acrobatics. During their aquatic courtship dance the salamanders may rub up against each other, but fertilization is an out-of-body experience for the male, who deposits his sperm in the pond. The female scoops up the sperm, fertilizes it, and lays her eggs, which hatch later in the season.

During the 1990s John Menke, a resident of Barnesville, noticed that many spotted salamanders were being killed on Route 109 as they tried to cross to a vernal pool on his property. Menke contacted the Maryland State Highway Administration, which agreed to study the problem and make changes in the road should they be warranted and feasible. A team of scientists and volunteers carefully studied the progress of the salamanders as they traveled to and from Menke's pond. The study did not result in changes to the road, but it provided young ecologists an opportunity for hands-on nature study.

Another common area salamander is the red-backed salamander *(Plethodon cinereus)*. It can be either all dark gray-black or dark with a red back. This salamander can be found in and under rotting logs and other cool, dark places in the woods.

6 Sugarloaf Country through the Seasons

Experiencing four distinct seasons is one of the great pleasures of living in a temperate climate such as the Mid-Atlantic region of eastern North America. In Sugarloaf country, the landscape undergoes dramatic transformations as the wheel of the year turns from winter to spring, to summer, and then to fall and winter again.

Familiarity with a place such as Sugarloaf creates a sense of intimacy much like the intimacy one feels with family and friends. While you can predict certain things about your loved ones, other things surprise you. So it is with the seasons. You can expect the winter to bring cold and frozen precipitation, but how much and when is anybody's guess. You can look forward to hearing the song sparrow sing during late winter, but will it be on the morning of February 26 or March 1 that you hear that first, crisp "maids, maids, maids, hang up your tea kettles, tea kettles, tea kettles"? You can look forward to seeing the pink lady's slippers in bloom during late April or early May, but how many of the twin green leaves appearing in early spring along Sugarloaf's trails will actually bear blossoms? And despite its distinct seasons, the Sugarloaf area is well known for the unpredictability of its weather.

What follows are descriptions of some of the natural events that those who live in the area or visit frequently take notice of as the year progresses. Because there are such diverse habitats in the landscape, residents and visitors are able to witness seasonal changes of extraordinary richness.

Winter

On or around the winter solstice, early risers in Sugarloaf country wake up to an ivory surprise. The world is still clad in its stark, post-autumn browns and grays, and the air is cold and raw. But on the horizon is a cheering sight: the small rounded mountain is dusted with the season's first snowfall.

The summit of Sugarloaf, which rises 800 feet from the surrounding countryside to an altitude of 1,282 feet above sea level, is usually two to three degrees cooler than the land around its base, explaining the early-winter dusting of snow. Throughout the winter, Sugarloaf and the surrounding Piedmont landscape receives intermittent snowfalls from fast-moving systems from the north and northwest and the occasionally heavy coastal storms.

Winter is a wonderful time to visit Sugarloaf Mountain, provided area roads are passable and safe. Following snowfalls, the gated road up the mountain is closed to vehicular traffic, sometimes for days, making the mountain a paradise for hikers, cross-country skiers, and seekers of solitude. The contoured quartzite rocks of Sugarloaf and the wind-sculpted table mountain pines at the summit are enhanced by the beauty of a fresh snowfall. The bare chestnut oaks creak in the winter wind, and you can hear the loud call of the pileated woodpecker long before the large black-and-white, red-crested bird flaps into view.

On cold, bright mornings, a hike to East View, West View, or the summit is rewarded with views of the snow-covered farmlands and villages below, reminiscent of paintings by Grandma Moses. A visit later in the day yields the rosiness of a winter sunset through bare trees. On overcast mornings the winter mood on Sugarloaf is very different. With the view obscured by a cloak of white cloud or mist, you feel sheltered and apart from the world. Perhaps a small warming trend has caused the snow-laden trees to drip, making spatter sounds on the rock. There is little wind on such a day, and suddenly a sound is heard, seemingly from another dimension. Is it children calling to one another, or foxes or hounds? Then a white V swoops in overhead through the mist: it is a flock of tundra swans flying over the mountain, conversing with one another in their otherworldly language.

Winter is a notoriously unpredictable season in Sugarloaf country. The season's contribution to the year's forty inches of precipitation can come in the form of cold rain and drizzle, sleet and freezing rain, snow (a foot of snow equaling a little over an inch of rain), or a mixture of all three, sometimes simultaneously! Whatever falls from the sky, anticipation of its arrival keeps schoolchildren and snow crews on high alert, wondering whether they'll have a day off or a night on, respectively. A few feet of elevation can turn a cold rain to ice or snow. What falls in Sugarloaf country often differs dramatically from what falls in the nation's capital, Baltimore, or even nearby Germantown.

For winter enthusiasts, Sugarloaf country is at its picturesque best after a heavy snowfall, especially when roads and airports have been forced to close. Many residents keep cross-country skis propped by the front door and are out gliding through the white world at the first opportunity. On the morning after a snowfall, the powdery gray-blue of the snow-laden mountain with white fields and red barns in the foreground is a sight to behold. And the silence of a landscape without planes and automobiles is transformational. On such a morning, the only noises come from the hungry flocks at the bird feeders and horses and other farm and wild animals testing the white powder.

For those who lack enthusiasm for winter, February brings a welcome sight. The intermittent thawing that has gone on all winter begins to reveal the brilliant, deepening green of Sugarloaf country's fields of winter wheat and rye. A few days or weeks later a joyous chorus arises from every pond and stream as the spring peepers (small treefrogs) begin their mating calls, a sound that has been likened to the ringing of sleigh bells. In late February and early March, male red-winged blackbirds begin flexing their scarlet wing patches while perched on tree branches, cattails, and telephone wires. Their hearty "conkarees" sound forth from every wetland, a sure announcement of spring.

There is another red blush on the landscape in the days preceding the spring equinox. The red maples begin to bloom, their tiny flowers adding a touch of red lace to the greening earth. Still another red, less obvious and more secretive, adorns the creeksides and springs of Sugarloaf and its surroundings: the strange wine-colored, hooded spathes of skunk cabbage flowers reward eagle-eyed "skunk hunters" who aren't afraid to get their feet wet. Chances are that a mourning cloak, spring's first butterfly, with its dark, yellow-trimmed wings, will float by on the first warm day of earliest spring.

Spring

Spring on Sugarloaf is one long, leisurely spell of flowering and leafing in which the weather is a potpourri of sun and rain, coolness and heat, breeziness and stillness. Beginning in March and continuing into June, the mountain's trails and roadsides are lined with a succession of spring blossoms. The greening trees fill with migrating and returning birds.

During early April, the rain-swollen tributaries of Bear Branch and Furnace Branch are lined with bright-green skunk cabbage leaves and the unfurling fronds of cinnamon ferns. Swallowtail butterflies dip and glide over the creek waters as newly returned ovenbirds call out "teacher, teacher, teacher" from the trees. As the trees leaf out during April and May, the mountain is transformed from its dramatic winter openness to a leafy cocoon. The tapered copper buds of the American beech swell to deliver their neatly veined leaves, and the witch hazels hold their scalloped-edged infant foliage to the sky. The deciduous trees growing up the mountain slopes flower and leaf, each species yielding its offering to the ephemeral spring palette of copper, bronze, gold, and green.[1]

Early spring is peak blooming time in area woodlands as flowering plants exploit the sunlight pouring onto the forest floor through leafless tree branches. Among the earliest of the mountain's spring flowers are bloodroot, yellow corydalis, cut-leaved and slender toothwort, round-lobed hepatica, rue anemone, and trailing arbutus, a sweetly scented, low-growing evergreen plant found along trails and roadsides. The fragrance of the small pink and white blossoms is well worth getting down on your hands and knees to experience. The earliest blooms are followed by jack-in-the-pulpit, wild geranium, violet wood sorrel, pink lady's slipper, showy orchis, and mayapple, to name but a few of Sugarloaf's spring wildflowers. Several species of violets, with blossoms ranging from white and purple to yellow, adorn Sugarloaf's trails. As you hike them in early spring, you will be treated to many other fragrant flowering trees, shrubs, vines, and herbaceous plants.

Spring is the season of returning and migrating birds, with peak migration lasting from mid-April to mid-May. One morning in a recent May, a birder recorded fifteen separate species of warblers along Mount Ephraim Road. Some—such as the black-and-white warbler, worm-eating warbler, and ovenbird—stay to nest on the mountain, while others continue on to nesting sites farther north. A spring hike is always a musical experience, and with a little persistence you can learn the songs and calls of some of the mountain's resident birds. (See pp. 70–72 for more on Sugarloaf's spring migrants and nesting birds.)

Late April and early May is high spring on Sugarloaf Mountain. The wood thrush, with its mystical flutelike song, is first heard in the mountain woodlands at the precise time the pink lady's slippers unfurl their pouchlike blossoms on tall stalks above paired, parallel-veined leaves. At this time the young leaves of the mountain's trees and shrubs are just reaching toward maturity.

High spring at Sugarloaf brings to mind Robert Frost's poem "Nothing Gold Can Stay," especially the poignant lines: "Nature's first green is gold / Her hardest hue to hold." There is such a sweetness in the tender shades of gold and green that climb Sugarloaf's slopes during early spring, and a sense of loss when the varied ephemeral hues settle down to a uniform green.

Watching mountain laurel buds unfold on Sugarloaf is a favorite ritual of frequent visitors. At first the buds are tiny and tightly braided, then they swell and grow pink. As the heat and humidity begin to rise in earnest, the mountain laurel blooms, blanketing Sugarloaf in pink and white snowball flower clusters above shiny evergreen leaves. The flowering mountain laurel is spring's dramatic farewell, a last gift of the season. From then on, woodland blossoming winds down a bit, while the summer flowers pop up in the fields ringing Sugarloaf's base. June is not without its woodland blooms. The curiously hooded flowers of several skullcap species bloom along the trails, as do the summer bluets called houstonia, the pasture rose, white avens, wild basil, and enchanter's nightshade. Near the summit on the Red Trail, the tall, creamy spikes of black cohosh emerge as spring gives way to summer.

Summer

In the valley below, the scent of Japanese honeysuckle is intoxicating. On early summer evenings the fireflies dance over the corn and wheat fields, and you may hear the once common, now all too rare song of the whip-poor-will. Around the summer solstice, a drive down West Harris Road from near the base of the mountain to the village of Barnesville is well worth your while. The road is lined with orange daylilies.

While woodland flowers are not as common in early summer, the fields and roadsides are brimming. Tall, white Queen Anne's lace and sky-blue chicory line area roads. Daisies, black-eyed Susans, yarrow, and hawkweed create splashes of color in the fields. Butterfly weed contributes an occasional dazzling orange; close inspection reveals this member of the milkweed genus to be teeming with the showy insects that give the plant its name. Wild fruits ripen everywhere: blueberries and huckleberries along mountain trails, and strawberries, cherries, black raspberries, blackberries, and wineberries in the woods, hedgerows, and fields. During early summer, the winter wheat and rye in the fields ringing Sugarloaf become "amber waves of grain," and picturesque barrel-shaped hay bales adorn area pastureland.

Maryland's summer heat and humidity are notorious. But on days when the air is clean, it can be pleasurable, especially since it invites indolence. These are days for fishing and canoeing on the Monocacy and Potomac Rivers or taking a picnic and a book to the top of the mountain, where it is always cooler and there may be a breeze drifting over the summit. A late lunch followed by a nap in the hammock with a cicada chorus would be a perfect agenda. Many Sugarloaf-area residents forego the comforts of air-conditioning, relying only on old-fashioned fans.

Steamy summer days often are punctuated by late-afternoon storms that can be dramatic. Black clouds roll over Sugarloaf, and thunder rumbles on the horizon. Heavy downpours, brilliant lightning bolts, high winds, and sometimes hail come roaring in from the west and then are gone. Sometimes the slowest moving storms linger through the night.

Several times each summer, most commonly in June and August, Canadian cold fronts break the heat and humidity, bringing a few consecutive days of clear, dry, low-humidity weather. These are kick-up-your-heels days. From the moment you awake with the sun until the crescent moon floats on a rosy horizon, there is not a cloud in the sky, and you are neither too hot nor too cold, but just right. If it has been humid for a length of time, with the fuzziness humidity brings to the horizon, these Canadian days will bring out the sharp contours of tree and sky. It's like wearing a new pair of glasses. Suddenly everything is sharply in focus, including the weeds in the garden!

Baltimore checkerspot butterfly

These are days to get out and pull those weeds, or to visit area farm stands or pick-your-own orchards. There is nothing like the first peach of the season, and farms on Peach Tree Road near Comus and Barnesville still produce them.

Toward late summer, when the insect choruses are deafening, there is a renewal of blossoming on the mountain itself. In August the cranefly orchid unfurls its small, greenish-purple, birdlike blooms along the trails. Members of the aster or daisy family predominate in August and September, with tall, dusky-purple joe-pye weed and yellow wingstem growing along wet areas of Mount Ephraim Road, and purple mistflowers, white boneset, and white snakeroot blooming along trails and roadsides. The mint family is well represented, too, including dittany, with its small purple flowers, branched, wiry stalk, and oregano-flavored leaves.

The floral stars of the season are the cardinal flowers in the springs and seeps of Sugarloaf. With a backdrop of royal and cinnamon fern, these crimson members of the *Lobelia* genus steal the show. A late-summer drive down Mount Ephraim Road is a chance to see the mountain's cardinal flowers in full bloom.

As the autumn equinox approaches and the days grow shorter, there is a bittersweet feeling in the air around Sugarloaf. But the year's best weather is just ahead.

Autumn

One day on or around the equinox, the heat and humidity are suddenly whisked away on a northwest wind and autumn comes to Sugarloaf country. The first visual sign is a blush in the tupelo trees. These common woodland trees turn peach, orange, scarlet, wine, or all four, heralding more widespread color to come. Tupelos are scattered throughout the woods on Sugarloaf, and their long-lasting color can be seen from every trail. The dogwoods that have survived the blight also turn an early red. During September the climbing vines of poison ivy and Virginia creeper ornament tree trunks with vivid color. The five-leafleted Virginia creeper turns crimson, while poison ivy turns red, orange, and yellow.

September weather is all over the map. The heat and humidity of the first part of the month alternate with cool, crystalline days. Some years, the remnants of hurricanes arrive, bringing several inches of rain, wind, and billowing tropical skies. As October nears, the days grow cooler and more brilliant. The blue profiles of Catoctin and South Mountains to the west stand out in sharp relief. Hawks fly over the summit of Sugarloaf on their fall migration.

Early fall is still prime wildflower season. Aster or daisy family members continue to bloom: this is the season for white, lavender, and purple asters, and for goldenrods. The graceful blue-stemmed goldenrod is common along mountain roads and trails, and several other species grow here, too. One member of the goldenrod genus blooming along Mount Ephraim Road bears white flower heads and goes by the poetic name silverrod. The white or pale pink turtlehead, a member of the snapdragon family and the only host plant for the rare Baltimore checkerspot butterfly (often known simply as the Baltimore), blooms in Sugarloaf's seeps and springs during September.

The primary botanical activity of early fall is fruiting. Acorns that have matured during the summer months suddenly fall from the oak trees, and you may wish you'd donned a hard hat before your hike.

Hickory nuts ripen and fall. The dogwood bears its small, scarlet drupes and the tupelo its sapphire ones; legumes hang from the redbud and black locust trees. Near Mount Ephraim Road, the red fruit of the spicebush, jack-in-the-pulpit, and false Solomon's seal contribute to Sugarloaf's autumn ambiance. The Indian cucumber root along moist sections of the Blue Trail bears purple-black berries above red leaf whorls.

Chipmunks, squirrels, and other small mammals gather and store Sugarloaf's fall fruits as they prepare for winter. Some of the mountain's creatures are headed for full hibernation, and this is a time when timber rattlesnakes or copperheads may be seen, especially on the western side of the mountain, as they return to their winter dens.

October is the mountain's most photogenic month, and that means crowds on beautiful weekends. During October and into early November the autumn foliage peaks: the ashes turn gold, bronze, and even purple; the tulip-trees and hickories glow yellow and gold; the maples and sassafras blaze red, orange, and yellow; and the oaks show everything from gold and copper to wine. The vivid color in the tupelos and dogwoods stays on the trees well into October. Daytime temperatures are often in the seventies or low eighties, and nights are deliciously chilly. Farm stands dazzle the eye with their piles of pumpkins and apples and signs for mouth-watering sweet cider. Area artists and artisans open their studios for the fall tour, displaying colorful skeins of home-spun wool and art inspired by the beauty of the landscape. October is usually the month of the first killing frost in Sugarloaf country, but sometimes it doesn't occur until November. It's been known to snow during October, with ripe tomatoes still on the vine.

As the flowering season winds down for another year, one small tree chooses late fall to burst into bloom. The witch hazels growing near Mount Ephraim Road, next to the stone steps of the Green Trail, and along other trails produce golden leaves and golden ribbonlike blossoms simultaneously. The blossoms remain on the trees after the leaves have fallen, sometimes into early winter.

November is an exhilarating time on the mountain. With most of the foliage gone, new and dramatic vistas open. The mountain's rocks, freed from summer shadows, sparkle in the late autumn sun.

There are still a few scarves of color here and there in the trees, and this is the month the red and scarlet oaks live up to their names. The October crowds are gone, and cooler temperatures make hiking a pleasure. Along Mount Ephraim Road, the American beech trees come into their winter beauty: smooth gray trunks and limbs and amber foliage that persists into the winter.

As the solstice draws near, the first winter sunsets enliven the skies with streaks of rose, red, orange, and purple, and snow lovers begin their annual vigil of amateur forecasting. Many city residents head out to Sugarloaf country to cut Christmas trees and purchase evergreen boughs for holiday decorating. As the shortest day approaches in Sugarloaf country, the wheel of the year is complete.

7 Saving Sugarloaf Country

On the wall of the Rockville, Maryland, post office is a mural of the Sugarloaf countryside painted by an artist named Judson Smith as a WPA project in 1940. The view looking toward the mountain from Comus is much the same view you see today. This is the result of careful rural land-use planning. When Tina Brown painted the picture used for the front cover of this book, she stood near the spot where Smith may have stood more than sixty years ago. You can see a rendition of Judson's mural below. Happily, the biggest change in the two scenes is in the size and shape of the hay bales!

The future of Sugarloaf depends on the careful stewardship of all who love it. When you come to Sugarloaf Mountain, think of what you can do to contribute to its well-being. Treat all plants and animals with respect. Consider volunteering for trail maintenance or making a contribution to Stronghold, Inc., the mountain's nonprofit caretaking trust.

As noted earlier, much of the farmland adjacent to Sugarloaf Mountain has been set aside by Montgomery County as an Agricultural Reserve, a model program in farmland conservation that has inspired other regions around the country.

While Frederick County has taken some steps to conserve the agricultural lands on the western side of the mountain, Montgomery County has been a pioneer in rural land preservation. Much of the land stretching below the mountain to the northeast, east, and south comprises a ninety-thousand-plus-acre Agricultural Reserve, in which

Sugarloaf Mountain from Comus (WPA mural in Rockville post office by Judson Smith, 1940). (Photograph courtesy of Stronghold, Inc.)

new residential building is restricted to twenty-five-acre lots. In 1980 a master plan for the county was devised in which rural landowners could sell transfer of development rights (TDRs) to property owners in designated urban and suburban areas. In addition, many Sugarloaf-area property owners—such as those who once owned the farmland pictured on our front cover—have signed conservation easements on their lands, restricting development even more in perpetuity.

While these land conservation efforts have become models for the nation—and the topic of classroom and council-room discussions across the country—the farms and villages of the Sugarloaf Mountain area are under siege. The stacks visible to the southwest from the mountain summit belong to a trash incinerator and a power plant near Dickerson. The mountain's "view shed" could soon include many more sights incompatible with the historic patchwork of farms and villages that is a poignant reminder of our agrarian past. Huge new projects that would destroy the rural character of the area are routinely proposed for Sugarloaf country. For many years, the base of Sugarloaf has been under consideration as a possible route for a multilane highway linked to a proposed new bridge across the Potomac.

Luckily, Sugarloaf country is blessed with many concerned citizens and tireless activists—a blend of longtime residents (many of them multigenerational) and newcomers who are united in their desire and willingness to protect their cherished farms and villages. Recently, local civic and environmental groups have joined with a large regional coalition whose mission is to fight sprawl and protect the integrity of the Washington metropolitan area's urban core, established suburbs, and precious green Montgomery County Agricultural Reserve. Those who love Sugarloaf Mountain can only hope that the spirit of preservation will prevail and that this still rural and scenic portion of Maryland's Piedmont will remain so for generations to come.

If you would like to become involved in the effort to preserve this precious rural legacy, consult the Friends of Sugarloaf Directory on page 102. You can make a difference by volunteering and/or contributing financial support to one or more of the organizations listed, and by writing letters to your elected representatives and newspaper editors urging preservation of the villages and farmlands that are still here for all to enjoy.

Notes

Introduction
  1. Gordon Strong, "Enjoyment of Beauty." Gordon Strong's writings, Stronghold, Inc.

1. The Geology of Sugarloaf Mountain
  1. A. J. Stose and G. W. Stose, "The Physical Features of Carroll County and Frederick County" (Baltimore: State of Maryland Board of Natural Resources, 1946); Alan Fisher, *More Country Walks Near Washington* (Baltimore: Rambler Books, 1985), pp. 174–79.
  2. Cynthia Shauer Langstaff interview, April 2001.
  3. Cristol Fleming, Marion Blois Lobstein, and Barbara Tufty, *Finding Wildflowers in the Washington-Baltimore Area* (Baltimore: Johns Hopkins University Press, 1995), p. 11.

2. The History of Sugarloaf Mountain
  1. Chris Haugh, *Monocacy: The Pre-History of Frederick County, Maryland* (film documentary, Chris Haugh, GS Communications, 1999).
  2. Frederick Gutheim, *The Potomac* (Baltimore: Johns Hopkins University Press, Maryland Paperback Bookshelf edition, 1986), p. 28. The first edition was published by Holt, Rinehart, and Winston in 1949 as part of the Rivers of America series.
  3. Ibid., p. 27.
  4. A good source for the history of early exploration and settlement of the Sugarloaf region is Grace L. Tracey and John P. Dern, *Pioneers of Old Monocacy: The Early Settlement of Frederick County, Maryland 1721–1743* (Bal-

timore: Genealogical Publishing, 1987; reprinted in 2002). History of quests for silver in the Sugarloaf area is recounted by Paul Thibault in *Sugarloaf: The Quest for Riches and Redemption in the Monocacy Valley* (film documentary, Chris Haugh, GS Communications, 2000).

5. Baron Christoph von Graffenried (1661–1743), "Christoph von Graffenried's Account of the Founding of New Bern" (Spartanburg, S.C.: Reprint Co., 1973), p. 384. Reproduced from a 1920 edition in the North Carolina Collection, University of North Carolina, Chapel Hill.

6. Sugarloaf Regional Trails, *Circling Historic Landscapes: Bicycling, Canoeing, Walking, and Rail Trails near Sugarloaf Mountain, Maryland* (Rockville, Md.: Sugarloaf Regional Trails and the Montgomery County Historic Preservation Commission of Maryland–National Capital Park and Planning Commission, second edition, 1999), p. 12.

7. Dona Cuttler and Michael Dwyer, *The History of Hyattstown* (Bowie, Md.: Heritage Books, 1998), p. 3.

8. Jackson Kemper III, *American Charcoal Making in the Era of the Cold-blast Furnace* (Hopewell Furnace National Historic Site: National Park Service, Eastern National Park and Monument Association, 1987; first published in 1941), p. 22.

9. Edward S. Delaplaine, *The Life of Thomas Johnson* (New York: Grafton Press, 1927); the files of the Montgomery County Historical Society and the files of the Historical Society of Frederick County; research by John Baines, Fawn A. E. Foerster, Glenn Cumings, and Ben Smart contributed to this history of the Johnson family at Sugarloaf.

10. Interview with Robert Kapsch, July 29, 2002.

11. Sugarloaf Regional Trails, *Circling Historic Landscapes*, p. 28.

12. Gutheim, *The Potomac*, p. 207.

13. Ibid.

14. Ibid., pp. 207, 208.

15. Ken Perkins research for Sugarloaf Regional Trails.

16. Ibid.

17. Gutheim, *The Potomac*, p. 210.

18. Folger McKinsey ("The Bentztown Bard"), "Sugar Loaf Mountain Has Seen History Pass below It," Frederick, Md.: *Frederick Post,* datelined Hyattstown, August 11, 1941.

19. Helen Urner Price, "Weird Mountain Beauty in New Park," Washington, D.C.: *Sunday Star,* July 17, 1932.

20. Ibid.

21. Stephen W. Sears, *Landscape Turned Red: The Battle of Antietam* (New Haven and New York: Ticknor and Fields, 1983), pp. 72–73.

22. Margaret Marshall Coleman, *Montgomery County: A Pictorial History* (Norfolk, Virginia Beach, Va.: Donning Co., revised edition, 1990), p. 40.

23. "Casualties of Battle" (Antietam National Battlefield printout, National Park Service). Some historians estimate higher fatalities.

24. Interview with Jacqueline Nichols, April 1997.

25. Stronghold, Inc., "The Strong Mansion on Sugarloaf Mountain," *Sugarloaf Mountain Newsletter,* Fall/Winter 1996, p. 1.

26. "Sugar Loaf Mountain," Frederick, Md.: *The Citizen,* September 30, 1904.

27. Price, "Weird Mountain Beauty in New Park."

28. "Sugar Loaf Mountain—'Stronghold,'" Frederick, Md.: Excerpts from *The Frederick News-Post 1942 Yearbook* (in the files of the Historical Society of Frederick County).

29. Letter from Gordon Strong to Frank Lloyd Wright, September 22, 1924, in Gordon Strong's papers at Stronghold, Inc.

30. Undated letter from Frank Lloyd Wright to Gordon Strong, in Gordon Strong's papers at Stronghold, Inc.

31. Letter from Gordon Strong to Frank Lloyd Wright, November 14, 1924, in Gordon Strong's papers at Stronghold, Inc.

32. Letter from Gordon Strong to Frank Lloyd Wright, October 14, 1925, in Gordon Strong's papers at Stronghold, Inc.

33. Letter from Frank Lloyd Wright to Gordon Strong, October 20, 1925, in Gordon Strong's papers at Stronghold, Inc.

34. Benjamin Forgey, "Something So Wright—The Architect's Brilliant, Unconstructed Ideas," *Washington Post,* November 16, 1996.

35. Helen Hammond, "Man of the Mountain," Frederick, Md.: *Frederick Magazine,* October 1994.

36. Gutheim, Frederick, *Remembering Gordon Strong,* unpublished, undated manuscript in the Frederick Gutheim collection of Jane C. Loeffler, Washington, D.C., p. 8.

37. Stronghold, Inc., "The Comstock School," *Sugarloaf Mountain Newsletter.* Editors: Linda Riggs and Ben Smart. Spring/Summer 1996.

38. Stronghold, Inc., "Gordon Strong—A Man and His Mountain," *Sugarloaf Mountain Newsletter,* Fall/Winter 1994.

39. Certificate of Incorporation of Stronghold, Incorporated, recorded with the state of Maryland, April 9, 1946.

40. Articles of Amendment of Stronghold, Incorporated, recorded with the state of Maryland, January 4, 1955.

41. Gutheim, *Remembering Gordon Strong,* p. 2.

42. Ibid., p. 7.

43. Stronghold, Inc., "Happy 50th Anniversary," *Sugarloaf Mountain Newsletter,* Fall/Winter 1996.

44. "Sugarloaf: A Monadnock for All Time," *Landmarks,* Maryland Environmental Trust Newsletter, vol. 1, no. 4 (article reprinted in *Sugarloaf Mountain Bulletin,* no. 29, 1987).

45. Stronghold, Inc., files.

46. Stronghold, Inc., "Frederick County Public Schools Educate at Sugarloaf Mountain," *Sugarloaf Mountain Newsletter.* Editors: Susan Dunn and David F. Webster. Spring/Summer 2002.

3. Sugarloaf's Trail System

1. James Alexander, "Sugar Loaf Mountain," *American Motorist,* May 1933.

5. Sugarloaf Wildlife

1. Claudia Wilds, *Finding Birds in the National Capital Area—Second Edition* (Washington, D.C., and London: Smithsonian Institution Press, 1992), p. 99.

6. Sugarloaf Country through the Seasons

1. Every year several hundred people awake before dawn on Easter morning to attend the sunrise service sponsored at East View by local congregations. As ministers and choirs lead the Easter celebration service, the first light of day spreads over the villages and greening farmlands of Comus, Barnesville, and beyond.

Suggested Reading

When Tina and I go into the field on Sugarloaf Mountain or elsewhere, we carry our favorite books with us. For casual wildflower walks we bring along *Newcomb's Wildflower Guide* (1977) by Lawrence Newcomb and Roger Tory Peterson and Margaret McKenny's *A Field Guide to Wildflowers* (1968). Both books are well illustrated—Newcomb's by Gordon Morrison and Peterson and McKenny's by Peterson. Newcomb's guide has a user-friendly botanical key. However, when the key fails us (as it does occasionally), we like to have Peterson's guide, which is organized by flower color, as a backup. When we are planning a day of serious botanizing, such as the many days that went into the creation of this book and our forthcoming companion volume, *An Illustrated Guide to Eastern Woodland Wildflowers and Trees: 350 Plants Observed at Sugarloaf Mountain, Maryland,* we schlep some fairly hefty tomes. We almost always carry Brown and Brown's *Herbaceous Plants of Maryland* (1984) and/or Strausbaugh and Core's *Flora of West Virginia* (1978). We usually bring along Gleason and Cronquist's *Manual of Vascular Plants* (1991), as well.

For tree identification, *The Complete Trees of North America* (2000) by Thomas Elias is a must. This comprehensive, simply worded, illustrated book can be used in the Florida Everglades, the Alaskan mountains, and just about everywhere else on the continent. Brown and Brown's *Woody Plants of Maryland* (1992 edition) is good for local trees and shrubs, and *Flora of West Virginia* covers woody plants as well as herbaceous ones. I also like to carry my own book *City of Trees: The Complete Field Guide to the Trees of Washington, D.C.* (1987), illustrated by my friend Polly Alexander.

When Tina and I are studying the medicinal uses of plants, *A Field Guide to Medicinal Plants and Herbs of Eastern and Central North America* (2000) by Steven Foster and James Duke is our bible in the field. Generally, we find the Peterson field guide series to be very good, including the guide to trees and shrubs, the guide to ferns, and the guide to birds. Another bird book I like to carry with me is the National Geographic Society's *Field Guide to the Birds of North America* (1987). The National Audubon Society's *The Sibley Guide to Birds* (2000), written and illustrated by David Allen Sibley, is an invaluable, up-to-date resource. My favorite butterfly book is *Butterflies through Binoculars* (1993) by Jeffrey Glassberg. We also consult *Field Guide to the Piedmont* (1997) by Michael A. Godfrey for information on regional wildlife.

Three titles are essential for any local naturalist's library. These are books that work well at home or in the field: *Finding Wildflowers in the Washington-Baltimore Area* (1995) by Cristol Fleming, Marion Blois Lobstein, and Barbara Tufty; *Finding Birds in the National Capital Area* (1992) by Claudia Wilds; and *Watching Nature: A Mid-Atlantic Natural History* (1997) by Mark S. Garland.

Maryland's Geology (1993) by Martin F. Schmidt Jr. is a readable guide to our state's geologic past and present. Alan Fisher describes geologic features of Sugarloaf in *More Country Walks Near Washington* (1985). My favorite local history book is *The Potomac* (1986) by Frederick Gutheim. Tina and I recommend the Sugarloaf Regional Trails publication *Circling Historic Landscapes: Bicycling, Canoeing, Walking, and Rail Trails near Sugarloaf Mountain, Maryland* (1999). Margaret Coleman's book *Montgomery County: A Pictorial History* (1990) paints a vivid portrait of the county's past. *Civil War Guide to Montgomery County, Maryland* (1996) by Charles T. Jacobs, *A Guide to Civil War Sites in Maryland—Blue and Gray in a Border State* (1998) by Susan Cooke Soderberg, and *Bicycling through Civil War History in Maryland, West Virginia, Pennsylvania, and Virginia* (1994) by Kurt B. Detwiler are among many good references available on regional Civil War history. *Saving America's Countryside: A Guide to Rural Conservation* (second edition, 1997) is a comprehensive handbook by Samuel N. Stokes, A. Elizabeth Watson, and Shelley S. Mastran. We also highly recommend two films available on video that were produced by Chris Haugh: *Monocacy: The Pre-History of Frederick County, Maryland* (1999) and *Sugarloaf: The Quest for Riches and Redemption in the Monocacy Valley* (2000).

We are indebted to all of the above sources and to the additional books and periodicals noted on pages 95–98 for the creation of this book.

Friends of Sugarloaf: A Directory

The following organizations are among those dedicated to protecting Sugarloaf Mountain and/or the surrounding farmland and villages.

Stronghold, Inc.
7901 Comus Rd.
Dickerson, Md. 20842
(301) 874-2024 or (301) 869-7846

Established by Gordon Strong in 1946, Stronghold is a private, nonprofit corporation that oversees the mountain and maintains its trails, facilities, and the Strong Mansion.

Conservation Organizations

Sugarloaf Citizens Association
Linden Farm
20900 Martinsburg Rd.
Dickerson, Md. 20842
(301) 349-4889

Sugarloaf Citizens Association is a nonprofit corporation representing more than a thousand families in a ninety-five-square-mile agricultural region adjacent to Sugarloaf Mountain. Formed in 1973, SCA is dedicated to the preservation of rural open space, resource conservation, and a clean environment.

Sugarloaf Regional Trails

Box 412

Barnesville, Md. 20838

Created in 1974, Sugarloaf Regional Trails is a nonprofit organization dedicated to the conservation of rural Montgomery County's cultural landscape. SRT has sponsored research, planning studies, and educational activities and has supported film and book projects.

Audubon Naturalist Society

8940 Jones Mill Rd.

Chevy Chase, Md. 20815

(301) 652-9188

E-mail: hq@AudubonNaturalist.org

Web site: AudubonNaturalist.org

Founded in 1897, the Audubon Naturalist Society of the Central Atlantic States is the Washington metropolitan region's oldest independent nonprofit environmental education and conservation organization, with a membership of more than ten thousand. The society's conservation program addresses environmental concerns in the Washington metropolitan area, including land use, water and air quality, and natural resource protection.

Chesapeake Bay Foundation

6 Herndon Ave.

Annapolis, Md. 21403

(410) 268-8833

Web site: www.cbf.org

One of the missions of the Chesapeake Bay Foundation is to work for the health of the bay by promoting sensible land-use solutions for the bay's watershed, which includes the Sugarloaf Region.

Coalition for Smarter Growth

1777 Church St., N.W.

Washington, D.C. 20036

(202) 588-5570

Web site: smartergrowth.net

With approximately forty member organizations, the Coalition for Smarter Growth is dedicated to preserving the quality of life in the

Washington region for current and future generations. Its mission includes protecting the city's urban core, fighting sprawl and promoting livable communities, improving mass transit systems, and preserving agricultural and natural areas.

F.A.R.M.: For a Rural Montgomery
P.O. Box 455
Poolesville, Md. 20837
(301) 916-3510
E-mail: f.a.r.m.@erols.com
Web site: www.zarnet.com/farm

F.A.R.M. is a nonprofit coalition of environmental, civic, agricultural, and preservation organizations whose mission is the protection of the nationally acclaimed Agricultural Reserve and its resources in Montgomery County.

Maryland League of Conservation Voters
One State Circle
Annapolis, Md. 21401
(410) 280-9855
Web site: mdlcv.org

The Maryland League of Conservation Voters is "the nonpartisan political voice of the environmental community." The Maryland LCV is dedicated to making environmental protection a top political priority.

Nature Conservancy
Maryland/D.C. Chapter
5410 Grosvenor Lane, Suite 100
Bethesda, Md. 20814
(301) 897-8570
Web site: tnc.org/maryland

The Nature Conservancy works to protect critical habitats for native plant and animal species.

1000 Friends of Maryland
1209 Calvert St.
Baltimore, Md. 21202
(410) 385-2910
Web site: friendsofmd.org
   A statewide coalition of business, preservation, community, and environmental organizations, 1000 Friends of Maryland fights sprawl while helping to revitalize older communities and protect rural areas and open space.

Sierra Club, Maryland Chapter
7338 Baltimore Ave., Suite 101 A
College Park, Md. 20740
(301) 277-7111
   The Maryland chapter of the Sierra Club works to protect Chesapeake Bay, curtail developmental sprawl, promote smart transportation, and protect family farms, among other environmental policy and educational initiatives.

Solutions Not Sprawl
1777 Church St., N.W.
Washington, D.C. 20036
(202) 588-5570
Web site: solutionsnotsprawl.org
   Solutions Not Sprawl is a regional alliance of civic and environmental organizations working to promote a sensible growth and transportation policy for the Washington region, including Montgomery County's Agricultural Reserve. The group's goal is to connect communities with smart transportation choices rather than new roads and bridges that foster sprawl.

Farmland Conservation

Several programs and agencies promote and administer farmland conservation near Sugarloaf. These include the Sugarloaf Countryside Conservancy, the Trust for Public Land (and other private easement programs), the Maryland Greenprint Program, the Montgomery County Agricultural Easement Program, the Maryland Environmental Trust, the Maryland Agricultural Land Preservation Foundation, and the Maryland-National Capital Park and Planning Commission (M-NCPPC), which administers several programs, including the Maryland Rural Legacy Program and the locally funded Legacy Open Space Program. To inquire about the Transfer of Development Rights Program or to learn about placing rural land in Montgomery County under a permanent conservation easement, contact Judy J. Daniel, AICP, at M-NCPPC: (301) 495-4559 or judy.daniel@mncppc-mc.org for referrals to direct contacts.

American Farmland Trust
1200 18th St., NW
Washington, D.C. 20036
(202) 331-7300
Web site: farmland.org
    This national organization is dedicated to farmland conservation.

Historic Preservation

Historic Medley District, Inc.
P.O. Box 232
Poolesville, Md. 20837
(Headquartered at the historic John Poole House and General Store Museum in Poolesville)
(301) 972-8588
    Founded in 1974, Historic Medley is a nonprofit historic preservation organization dedicated to preserving historic structures and open space in western Montgomery County.

The above list is but a sample of the many fine organizations working to protect the integrity of the Sugarloaf region.

Index

Italicized page numbers refer to illustrations